D1062784

Literacy in Action

Literacy in Action

by

**David Wray,
Wendy Bloom and
Nigel Hall**

The Falmer Press
(A member of the Taylor & Francis Group)
London ● New York ● Philadelphia

UK   The Falmer Press, Falmer House, Barcombe, Lewes, East Sussex, BN8 5DL

USA   The Falmer Press, Taylor & Francis Inc., 242 Cherry Street, Philadelphia, PA 19106–1906

© D. Wray, W. Bloom and N. Hall

All rights reserved. No part of this publication may be reproduced, stored in a retrieval system, or transmitted, in any form or by any means, electronic, mechanical, photocopying, recording, or otherwise, without permission in writing from the Publisher.

First published 1989

British Library Cataloguing in Publication Data

Wray, David, 1950–
  Literacy in action.
  1. Great Britain. Children. Literacy. Development
  I. Title II. Bloom, Wendy III. Hall, Nigel
  302.2'0941
  ISBN 1-85000-604-0
  ISBN 1-85000-605-9 pbk

Typeset in 11/13 Garamond by
Bramley Typesetting Limited, 12 Campbell Court, Bramley, Basingstoke, Hants. RG26 5EG

Jacket design by Caroline Archer

Printed in Great Britain by Taylor & Francis (Printers) Ltd, Basingstoke

ROBERT MANNING
STROZIER LIBRARY

APR 11 1990

Tallahassee, Florida

LB
1576
W69
1989

Contents

Preface

This book is about literacy in the primary years of schooling, from nursery school to the end of the junior school. Its chief concern is to explore the ways in which teachers go about developing the literacy of the children under their charge. It aims to give its readers the opportunity to look very carefully at the context and the content of literacy programmes. This starting point of actual practice in teaching literacy is deliberate. It is only, we believe, from a thorough examination of what already happens that teachers can begin to sensibly develop their practice.

The book is based on a general philosophy of literacy education which can be summed up as follows:

(a) All children with normal facility in the use of language can become literate given the opportunity.

(b) In the same way that learning language is about using language, so becoming literate is about using literacy.

(c) The adults who are most useful to children are those who *facilitate* the development of literacy rather than *instruct* children in it.

(d) The development of literacy is fostered by appropriate contexts.

How to Use the Book

This book is a little different from others you may have read on similar topics. It is not designed to be read straight through without pause. It is possible to treat it this way, and we have provided the necessary support for this where possible, but reading it this way would be to miss its most important feature. It is conceived as an 'interactive' book, which means that throughout it needs some response from you, its reader. This response will often be some form of observation since, as we said above, we believe the best starting point for thinking about what might happen in classrooms is a close examination of what already does. We will often ask you to examine classrooms and children in the light of points we make, and also to put forward your own explanations of and suggestions for classroom practice. We hope it will be possible at regular intervals for you to discuss the observations and suggestions you make with other readers of the book. This will certainly enrich your experience of the book.

The Structure of the Book

We have followed a developmental structure in the book, with its major part being a chronological look at the literacy development of children in the primary years. Chapter 3 focuses on the beginnings of literacy in the pre-school and nursery years, a time whose importance in the growth of literacy we are only just beginning to understand. Chapter 4 looks at the infant school, the traditional time of introduction to reading and writing. Chapters 5 and 6 take us forward into the lower and upper junior schools respectively when the emphasis tends to shift from the learning of, to the learning through, literacy.

Before this, however, Chapter 1 looks at the nature of literacy in the world outside school and the implications this might have for its treatment within school. Chapter 2 is a crucial one in that it introduces the process of careful observation of the literacy dimensions of classrooms.

An important feature of the book is its annotated bibliography. This book is only a starting point for an understanding of the development of literacy, and there are many others which would be interesting and useful follow-up reading.

Chapter 1

Literacy as a Social Experience

Introduction

We live in a literate society. This observation is so obvious as to be almost fatuous. Yet its implications for teachers and schools concerned with helping their children to develop literacy are far-reaching. If the process of schooling is seen as, at least partly, a preparation for, and a complement to, life in the world outside school, then it matters a great deal how schools reflect the literate environment from which their children come and in which they live and grow. One of the chief aims of this book is to examine the experience of literacy which children get in their schools and to question whether it is as full as it might be or as representative of literacy as possible. The first step towards this is to examine what literacy actually means for participants in modern society, and the range of ways in which literacy is used in everyday life.

The first point to make is that it is difficult to envisage a life without literacy. It is such a central part of our lives that we scarcely, in fact, notice it. Yet we have only to ask those unfortunate people who, for one reason or another, never quite master the complexities of literacy, to realize that so much of what we take for granted is crucial for comfortable survival in our world. The signs are all around us.

We wake in the morning, brush our teeth using toothpaste from tubes covered in print. We eat our breakfasts, using food from packets and cartons similarly covered with print. We catch up on the daily news using print, we may cook using a recipe involving print. We catch buses and trains to go to work, and use print to guide us to correct places. If we drive we use the print on traffic signs to direct us, and to learn to drive in the first place we had to be expert print users, if only to fill in the licence application form. At work all of us use print in some ways. We read: signs, rules, instructions, articles, memos, notices, books. We write: letters, notes, memos, diagrams, jottings. We go shopping and pick our way through a bombardment of print which informs, persuades, directs, and entertains us. At home we use print for leisure, from finding the times of our favourite TV programmes to immersing ourselves in our current novel. We pay bills, write shopping lists, read bank statements, write letters, read magazines etc. In addition, the institutions in which we work, and which surround us, are organized around literacy. Society would grind to a halt if orders were not processed, receipts given, memos passed, laws printed, timetables designed. The so-called paperless office is even farther off than when microcomputers began to be used by commerce and industry. Almost all social, commercial, industrial and political transactions are mediated by literacy. Small wonder that people who have problems with the processes of reading and writing feel cut off and helpless in this literacy-dense environment.

It cannot be said that things are getting simpler. Not only are there new experiences with print to cope with, from computers to bank cash machines, from railway announcement video screens to fax, but the level of operation demanded by everyday print is increasing. To take a commonly cited example, the informal benchmark for literacy twenty years ago was the ability to read and understand the daily newspaper (*The Daily Mirror*), which demanded a reading level equivalent to that of the average 9 to 10-year-old. Today that same newspaper demands a reading level of 14 to 15 years. Schools clearly need to take into account these trends if they are to continue to achieve the success they have achieved in the past.

What Do We Mean By Literacy?

The first step to take is to examine what literacy actually involves. You might like to spend some time thinking about what you understand by the term 'literacy'. What would you expect a 'literate person' to be like and to be able to do? The following three short quotations taken from a much more detailed examination of these concepts might give you some starting points.

> The classical definition of literacy as embracing the domain of high culture fails to address our situation, and we no longer accept its implicit associations linking literacy with an esoteric lettered class.

Literacy is:

the ability to respond to the practical tasks of everyday life, the ability to read and write a simple message.

Being 'literate' has always referred to having mastery over the process by means of which culturally significant information is coded.

(Quotations taken from de Castell, Luke and Egan, 1986)

Doing Things With Print

A common-sense definition of literacy may simply be that it consists of activities involving print. The emphasis here is on the physical actions associated with literate behaviour. Of course, literacy does involve some physical actions such as the use of one's eyes and hands, but this is a comparatively minor aspect of the process. The processes which take place inside the head are clearly much more crucial. Yet it is very common for people, including teachers, to make judgments about others' mastery of literacy on the basis of what they are seen to do. If we see someone reading a book by flicking through the pages one after another fairly rapidly, we tend to judge that he is not reading very thoroughly. If we see a child reading who points laboriously at every individual word with his/her finger, we judge him/her not to be a very skilled reader. We are all influenced in our judgments of people's writing abilities by what their writing looks like on the page. Neatly written script impresses us more than scribbled work.

Interestingly enough, this attention to the physical manifestations of literacy, rather than its internal processes, is reflected in young children's early concepts of literacy. One of us studied the responses of nursery children to the questions, 'Can animals learn to read?', and 'Can animals learn to write?' (see Hall (1988) for a fuller account of this study). These children seemed to associate reading and writing much more with physical actions than with any internal process.

If we reject the 'physical actions' definition as being inadequate, what other kinds of definitions might we consider? Thinking back to the three quotations we gave earlier, you might like to spend some time considering these questions.

Is the term 'literate' as applied to a person synonymous with 'cultured', or 'educated'?

Is a literate person necessarily a good citizen?

Literacy in Action

Does being literate imply any degree of self-determination, or are these concepts not really linked?

Can a computer be literate?

Compare your thinking on these questions with the points we make below. Because these are controversial issues, there is clearly no single 'right' answer to any one of them, yet answers you give may well have major implications for your approach to literacy in the classroom.

Literacy as Culture

In our everyday use of language we commonly use the term 'literate' in similar ways to 'educated' or 'cultured'. We might say things such as 'These children come from a highly literate home background', or 'This man is extremely literate. He seems to have read everything'. The term here means more than simply reading and writing, but has implications of some kind of quality.

This usage stems from the historical development of literacy. We are so accustomed nowadays to literacy being a more or less universal phenomenon, that it is difficult to appreciate that for hundreds of years it was not. Before the invention of the printing press, literacy was very much the preserve of an elite. The position of scribe was one with a high degree of status because the skills it demanded were in short supply. Reading and writing were not skills possessed by the majority of the population, but were concentrated in certain groups. Religious groups used them to preserve and embellish sacred works. Other written materials, because they were painstaking to produce, were scarce and expensive and therefore the preserve of those with sufficient resources.

The elitist view of literacy was, in fact, vigorously upheld by some groups who saw it as positively harmful for ordinary people to be 'taught their letters'. If they could read, they could then read works such as the Bible for themselves, and then would not need the church to interpret it for them. The universalization of literacy, through the spread of printing, was for many people a highly political process.

The effect of the introduction of printing was to make the elitist view of literacy increasingly untenable. The more people had reading and writing available to them, the more they came to involve themselves in it, and in the end rely upon it. The spread of literacy made for a more complex society which, in turn, demanded greater mastery of literacy. Universal literacy became essential for the effective functioning of society. One of the chief motivating forces behind universal education was the need for literate workers. The three Rs were given the central position in education that they have occupied ever since. In more recent times the degree of literacy in a country has come to be a measure of the civilization of that country. Revolutions in countries such as Russia, China and Cuba have had as one of their chief aims the spread of literacy. Literacy is no longer elitist but universal.

Literacy and Citizenship

As we have just argued, modern society needs people with sufficient command of literacy to act as good and useful citizens. This idea, however, requires further analysis. What does being a 'good citizen' involve? Where does literacy fit into this?

You might spend a few minutes now considering what your citizenship involves. If you think of this in terms of the roles a citizen plays in society, you might come up with a list similar to that below.

A useful citizen may be involved in any or all of these roles:

  (i)   creating a stable environment for the upbringing of
        future citizens;
 (ii)   contributing to society through work;
(iii)   participating in education and training processes;
 (iv)   contributing to the running of society by paying taxes
        etc.;
  (v)   helping select the administrators of society through
        the democratic process;
 (vi)   using the goods that are produced in society;
(vii)   using non-working time in positive ways.

You might be able to add further roles to this list.

A grouping of these roles gives five basic areas in which citizens are involved (Merritt, 1973).

1 Home and family
2 Employment and education
3 Community and government
4 Consumer
5 Leisure

The use of literacy has an essential place in each of these areas. Take each of these areas in turn and list some of the ways in which you use literacy to fulfil roles in this area.

Compare your own list with the list below and note any important areas of difference.

1 *Home and family*
Reading recipes, reading instructions for domestic appliances, reading child care books, reading about family health care, reading letters from family members, writing letters to friends and relations, filling in social security claim forms, etc.

2 *Employment and education*
Reading textbooks, reading journal articles, reading job advertisements, filling in application forms, writing essays, writing school records, etc.

3 *Community and government*
Reading rate demands, reading community newsletters, reading election leaflets, filling in tax forms, writing to members of Parliament, taking the committee minutes for local groups, etc.

4 *Consumer*
Reading advertisements, reading mail order catalogues, reading credit card statements, writing shopping lists, writing letters of complaint to suppliers, applying for extended credit, etc.

5 *Leisure*
Reading holiday brochures, reading a novel, reading a cordon bleu cookery guide, filling in a holiday booking form, writing postcards, keeping notes of photographs taken and camera settings, etc.

You are likely to find that any use you make of literacy can be fitted under one of these headings, although there will, of course, be some overlap. For example, you may classify reading a holiday brochure under leisure, but it might go equally well under consumer. This does not matter terribly, as the point of this exercise was to give you an idea of the spread of literacy uses across your life.

The results give rise to the question of how this analysis is reflected in the literacy experience of children in school. We shall discuss this issue later in this chapter, but at this point you might like to consider these questions.

Is it desirable for children to have experience in school of using literacy for this range of purposes?

Is this feasible? We would probably not want to involve primary school children in filling in tax forms, but might there be equivalent activities which have real relevance to their roles as citizens?

Can you suggest ways of widening children's experiences of literacy in school?

Literacy and Self-determination

The idea that a person needs to be literate in order to be a good citizen is subject to the very powerful criticism that it sees literacy as an essentially passive thing. If individuals are thought of as existing to serve society's needs and to fit in with its demands, literacy can be seen as one device for controlling them. This concept is central to the work on literacy of Paulo Freire and his associates (Freire, 1972). Literacy is, according to Freire, predominantly used as a mechanism of social control. Those agencies in society which seek to control others, either governments, companies or other associations, in fact require certain minimal levels of literacy in those they control. The mechanisms of social control in modern society depend upon literacy. Propaganda, rules, regulations, publicity of various forms all use print and depend upon the population's ability to decipher that print.

Literacy, however, can be defined as involving much more than this passive approach. An earlier definition of literacy claimed that it involved 'having mastery over the process by means of which culturally significant information is coded'. If this is accepted it implies that the literate person, far from being controlled by the manifestations of literacy, is, in fact, in control of them. This involves having some autonomy in the process of using literacy, and having the ability to make choices. Propaganda and publicity rely for their effect upon recipients' lack of autonomy, and their sometimes overpowering influence upon the choices made.

But what precisely is it about literacy that demands this autonomy and ability to make choices? An interesting insight into this question can be gained if we consider the case of the computer (Wray, 1988). Is it possible to describe a computer as literate? Computers can clearly read to an extent, since they can make a response if we type a statement or question into them. They can print, since they produce most of our bills, and those personalized invitations to enter various competitions or purchase goods which we regularly find in our mail. Is this sufficient to make them literate?

You might like to spend some time considering and discussing this issue. Try to list some of the activities which computers can do which can be described as literate behaviour. Then try to list some things which you think you do as a literate person which a computer cannot do.

It is clear that computers can be very good at some tasks which we would have to agree involve elements of literacy. They can hold and keep tabs on vast collections of information items. They can sort through these for particular items very quickly. They can assemble together discrete items with common features. They can respond to instructions and learn from them. They can reject certain inputs as nonsensical, irrelevant, less worthwhile or unsubstantiated. They can communicate by outputting written information in a variety of formats, matched to the particular task in hand, to anywhere in the world equipped with another computer and a telephone line. Many of these things they can do far better than any human being. These tasks clearly involve reading, writing and the handling of information, all of which are part of literacy.

There are, however, two vital things which computers cannot do which are an integral part of literacy. These are to do with setting purposes and making evaluations.

When we listed above the 'literate' things which computers can do, we did not mention the feature implicit in all of these: that is that computers can only do these things when they have been told to. Computers follow sets of instructions (programs) and, although these instructions can be extremely complex, they are given to the computer, not generated by it. Human use of literacy is occasionally like this. We sometimes simply read and write what and how we have been told. But we can do more than this. We can choose our own purposes for reading, writing and handling information. What these purposes might be we shall discuss later, but the important point at this juncture is our ability to determine purpose. It is partly this which gives us our autonomy in the use of literacy, and it is something which computers cannot do.

A further thing which is difficult for computers is the evaluation of information. They do, of course, make evaluations, but again only in accordance with the instructions they have been given. In the early days of the use of computers, it was known for people to receive computer-generated bills for £0, or worse, for £1,000,000. These were usually attributed to computer error, when in fact they were nothing of the kind. Because computers can only act on instructions, they can only evaluate mistakes if they have been alerted to them through these instructions. Mistakes made are therefore not the fault of the computer, but the computer programmer. This principle is so well known in the computer world as to have an acronym assigned to it: GIGO — Garbage In, Garbage Out.

Human beings are not limited in this way in their abilities to make evaluations of information they deal with. They can generate their own criteria for evaluation, some of which, indeed, need not be 'logical' in the computer's sense of the word. This ability to evaluate enables literate humans to deal with propaganda, publicity etc., and is a crucial element in the view of literacy as a process involving autonomy.

These two features of full literacy, the ability to decide for ourselves what our purposes for reading and writing will be, and the ability to evaluate what we read and write, are central to the view of literacy as an autonomous process, which involves having 'mastery over the process' of information coding.

Literacy and Motivation

So far we have discussed the abilities which are involved in literacy, but have said little about what might be termed the affective side of literacy. This is certainly an issue for debate. Should we apply the term 'literate' to people who *can* do all the things associated with literacy, but decide they do not wish to? It has long been argued that the term 'educated' implies not just a mastery of knowledge and skills but also the acceptance of a set of values, these values implying a belief that being educated is a worthwhile thing to be (Peters, 1966). Applying the same argument to literacy, it might be seen to imply a belief in the value of being literate. It would be difficult to conceive of anyone who valued literacy yet did not choose to use it.

The issue is of greater importance than a mere debating point. It is very common indeed to find products of our educational system who are quite able to use literacy when they need to, but who do not choose to very often. Many children are reluctant readers for whom reading holds no interest whatsoever, and who will scarcely ever voluntarily read a book, especially a work of fiction. Most teachers will recognize children like this in their own classes, and it would be an unusual teacher who did not feel some sense of having failed with these children. Reluctant writers are probably even more common, yet do not occasion the same sense of failure. Yet if children come through school without a feeling that it can be interesting and enjoyable to write, this seems just as much a case of failure on the school's part as if they have no interest in reading. We might, then, include in our understanding of the meaning of literacy an appreciation of the importance of motivation and the willingness to engage in it.

What Is Literacy?

It would be useful at this point if, taking into account all the points we have made so far, you were to attempt to formulate your own definition of what literacy is. In the final chapter of the book we give the definition which we have been working to. Compare your own definition with this. Any areas of difference will give a useful focus for debate.

How Do We Use Literacy In Our Lives?

In the previous section the point was made that, as inhabitants of a literate society, we use literacy all the time in our daily lives, at work, school, or at leisure. In this section we shall examine the ways in which we use literacy and any aspects these seem to have in common. We shall begin by looking at the actual literacy events in our lives.

Think back over your experience over the last seven days. Make a note of as many times as you can remember when you engaged in literate behaviour, either by reading, writing or handling information. You may find that this task is not as simple as it appears, firstly because much of the literate behaviour we engage in is so taken for granted it is difficult to actually remember it, and secondly because, if we do begin to remember literacy events over a period such as a week, the task becomes almost impossible due to the sheer number of such events. It would not be unusual to have over fifty events in your list, but you will need at least ten for the next activity. Compare your list with that of a friend or colleague. This may jog your memory and prompt you to add to it.

Next, go through your list and pick out the first five events which involved mainly reading. Now pick out the first five which involved mainly writing. For each of these ten events, write some brief notes in answer to the following questions.

(i) Why did you do this?
(ii) How did you set about the task?
(iii) What happened as a result?
(iv) What format was the material with which you were working?

Compare your answers with those of other people. Does this analysis raise any issues in your mind? If so, you might make a brief note of them and compare them with our comments below.

When one of us did this activity we came up with the following list of events and analysis. How does it compare with yours?

Reading Events

The morning newspaper

I began doing this to find out what had happened in the world recently, and also to find out the weather forecast for the day.

I initially glanced quickly over the headlines on the first three pages of the paper, before stopping to read one report which particularly interested me in more detail. When I finished that, I glanced quickly at the back page until I found the weather forecast for my area, which I read more slowly.

I had a conversation later at work about the report I had read in detail, so I suppose I must have actually learnt something from it. When I got into the car I checked to see that my umbrella was on the back seat as rain was forecast.

The newspaper format is quite distinctive.

The telephone bill

I read this to find out how much it was for.

I glanced quickly over the bill to see the amount owed.

I actually paid the bill four days later.

Again bills have a very distinctive format.

The minutes of a committee I serve on

I read these to refresh my mind before the next committee meeting that afternoon.

I read quickly to get the gist of what the minutes covered, but read one particular item much more slowly.

Literacy in Action

As a result of my reading I made a few quick notes of some issues to bring up at the meeting.

Loose leaf paper, written in the distinctive minutes format.

Three application forms from candidates for a course I teach

I read these to decide which candidates we should offer interviews to.

I skimmed over parts of the forms, but read parts in more detail, especially the enclosed references.

I decided that we should interview two of the candidates, and passed on a note to that effect to my secretary.

Standard application form format.

A journal article

I read this to check if it would be any use in some research I was planning.

I read through it very quickly at first, looking for any references to the particular topic I was interested in. I could not find any which seemed really interesting, but I did see a quotation which seemed useful so I read that carefully and looked in the bibliography to check where it came from.

I crossed the article off my list of possible sources of information, but later on I followed up the new reference it had given me.

Usual journal format.

Writing Events

A cheque to pay my credit card bill

I wrote this to pay the bill before they began to charge me interest.

I filled in the cheque and the payment slip apart from the day's date, which I had to look up in the newspaper, and then come back to.

The bill was paid.

Both cheque and payment slip are in characteristic format.

A letter to my brother

I wrote this to keep in contact and because it was my turn to write.

I wrote the first page very fast, almost scribbling. I then took much longer over the next page, pausing almost between each word, before finishing off in a rush.

I posted the letter and received a reply some time later.

Letter format.

A form to apply for a place at a conference
I wrote this because I particularly wanted to attend the conference.

I filled this in steadily, but had to stop to look in my diary before filling in my home telephone number, which is new.

I sent off the form and am looking forward to the conference.

A fairly straightforward form format.

A comment sheet for a student teacher's lesson I had watched the previous day
I wrote this to provide myself and the student with a written record of the points we had discussed after the lesson.

I wrote this very slowly, with a great deal of thought going into every word. I broke off in the middle of it to talk to a visitor.

When I had finished I decided that I would need to arrange to see the student to discuss what I had written.

Loose leaf paper, three pages of connected prose.

This chapter
I wrote this to introduce some of the chief themes of this book, and because it was the next thing on my agenda.

This was written over several days. Some parts were written very quickly, but others were very laborious. There were many times when nothing was actually written on paper at all, although I was thinking hard about it. Several sections I had written were deleted, and others substantially rewritten.

The outcome is what you are now reading.

Book format.

This survey is not, of course, very scientific, and the points we make below may seem to be based upon some fairly flimsy evidence. If you combine the analysis you have done of your own literacy events with that of several colleagues, you may get a much more reliable picture. This will give you the material for a very productive comparison with the general points we make about the use of literacy in our everyday lives.

There seem to be four major points about literacy which emerge from this analysis, which we shall discuss in more detail. These are:

(a) literacy is almost always used purposefully;
(b) both reading and writing involve the use of several different strategies;

(c) literacy usually has some kind of outcome;

(d) literacy involves the use of a range of distinct formats.

As we discuss these points you might consider how they relate to the experience of literacy which children commonly get in classrooms. We shall discuss this in the final section of this chapter.

Literacy is Purposeful

Very occasionally people engage in literacy with no apparent purpose. While sitting in the doctor's waiting room, I might pick up a magazine and idly flick through it with no need to gain anything from it at all. While listening to a lecture which is less than riveting, I might absent-mindedly scribble words and phrases on my note pad. These occasions are very few in number, however, and are far outnumbered by my normal use of literacy, which is with a clear purpose in mind.

What kinds of purposes do we commonly have for using literacy? Look back through your analysis of literacy events and your responses to the question, 'Why did you do it?' Can you think of any way of classifying your purposes? Compare your classification with that given below.

The purpose which probably emerges most readily is to do with the passing on of information. We use literacy both to send and receive items of information. We write to tell other people things we want them to know. As one child once wrote, 'We write because other people cannot read our minds'. We read to get information, and usually we have a reasonably clear idea of what information we want before we begin reading.

The other kind of purpose which you probably picked out more easily in your reading than your writing is that concerned with simple enjoyment. We often do read for pleasure, when the information we derive is not important, but the experience of reading is. This purpose is rather harder to find in relation to writing. For many people writing is simply a chore which they will only do if there is a good reason, and is rarely something they do for enjoyment. There are, of course, many others for whom writing itself can be a source of pleasure. For people like ourselves, for example, the chief reason for writing is to tell people things, but we do get a great deal of pleasure from it as well, especially when we finish it!

Most adult use of literacy can be fitted into these two purpose areas, the functional and the recreational. Is the same true of children's use of literacy in schools?

Literacy Involves a Range of Strategies

In your descriptions of the way you went about your literacy tasks, you probably noticed that you had no single way of proceeding. You in fact had a range of strategies for reading and writing. Taking reading and writing separately, can you classify in any way the strategies you used? You will probably have found that there was not a one-to-one match between individual tasks and strategies, but that you switched between strategies as you performed each task.

In reading, you may have been able to identify three distinct strategies. The obvious one, which in fact you probably used least of all, is reading every word carefully and intensively. This intensive reading is used when we want to make absolutely sure we follow the argument we are reading, or when we are trying to absorb and remember everything in a particular text. Reading would be a very laborious process if this was the only strategy we had. Unfortunately for some people, it sometimes is, which might explain their unwillingness to engage in it.

A much more commonly used strategy is what is known as skimming. In this we glance over texts very quickly simply to get a general impression of what they are about. Most people use this strategy to read novels for pleasure. This is a mathematical necessity. We could measure the time it takes a fluent reader to recognize individual words, then multiply this time by the number of words in a novel. This would give a time for reading the novel at least three and probably more times as long as it would actually take. Skimming over a text to get the gist of it is a natural way of reading, although obviously people vary in their skill at doing it. Techniques of so-called 'speed reading' develop the ability to skim read. Skimming is used in reading other kinds of material than novels. It is commonly used in studying when we glance over material to get the general idea of it and assess whether we should read it in detail. Notice the way in which skimming and intensive reading interact with each other.

A third strategy you are likely to have employed is known as scanning. This occurs when a reader searches a text for a particular detail. It is the strategy which is used when looking for a name in a telephone directory and again people vary in their skill at doing it.

Notice how, in reading, the strategies employed vary according to the purposes the reader has. If you go to a text looking for a particular detail, for example, the date of the Battle of Waterloo, it only makes sense to use the scanning strategy. Anything else would be inefficient. If your purpose is different, say to learn a poem off by heart, then skimming and scanning alone are not likely to be efficient strategies. Most purposes for reading are more complex than these, and the use of a variety of strategies will be demanded, although the reader still needs to know when to switch to particular ones.

With writing, strategies can generally be distinguished in terms of pace. Sometimes the writer may proceed at a steady even pace, but this is quite unusual. An erratic pace is more common. This is brilliantly captured in the mock sports commentary on Thomas Hardy's beginning to write *The Return of the Native* broadcast by the Monty Python team (1973):

> *Commentator*:
>
> And he's off! It's the first word — but it's not a word. Oh no! It's a *doodle* way up on the top of the left-hand margin; it's a piece of *meaningless* scribble. And he's signed his name underneath it. Oh dear, what a disappointing start! But he's off again, and here he goes: the first word — at 10.35 on this very lovely morning. It's three letters; it's the definite article; and it's *the*! . . . But he's crossed it out! . . . the *only* word he's written so far — and he's . . . But he's . . . No, he's down again and writing . . . He's written 'the' again — he's crossed it out again, and he's written 'a'. And there's a second word coming up straight away, and it's 'sat'. 'A sat'? Doesn't make sense. 'A Satur'? 'A Saturday' . . . And it's 'afternoon'. 'A Saturday afternoon' — it's a confident beginning. And he's straight into the next word — it's 'in'. 'A Saturday afternoon in . . .' In . . . in . . . in . . . 'No . . .' — Novembr? November's spelt wrong: he's left out the second 'e'. But he's not going back — it looks as though he's going for the *sentence*! . . .

Although satirical, this is in fact typical of writing. Strategies in writing range from the extremely slow, each word followed by long thinking time, to the very fast, when we degenerate to scribbling to keep up with the flow of ideas. At other times we may deliberately process and sift the ideas we write, and produce a series of notes which may have little meaning for outsiders.

As with reading, purpose interacts with strategy. If we are writing to produce a definite impression on our readers, we are likely to weigh up our words more carefully. In writing purely to remind ourselves, however, choice of words will take up less time and our writing will be speedier.

Literacy has an Outcome

As a corollary to the fact that the vast majority of literacy events have a purpose, they also have some kind of result. It is quite difficult to think of engaging in any literate behaviour which does not have a result, ranging from physical action to the bringing on of a particular emotional state. Think back to the literacy events you analyzed earlier. Were there any which had no result at all? Can you classify the results they had in any way?

One of the commonest results of literacy is physical action. There are many examples of this. If we read something we may do something as a result. Reading a recipe may result in cooking, reading instructions in constructing, reading a text book in writing, and reading a letter in replying. Writing may also result in action. Sometimes we may do something ourselves as a result of our own writing. The process of writing a shopping list may determine what we buy in the shop, or we may jot down a note to ourselves which later prompts us to do something. More commonly, though, what we write has an effect upon the physical actions of other people. Upon reading our letter a friend may write back, a visitor may follow our written directions to find us, or a child may begin an activity after reading a worksheet we have written. Results of this kind may be referred to as behavioural outcomes.

Another common result of literacy is an increase in knowledge or understanding. As a result of reading we may learn something we did not know before. This is one of the chief reasons why we read, and does not only apply in educational contexts. We read train timetables to learn when a train departs, we read guidebooks to learn about places we will visit, and newspapers to learn about events in the world. Things may also be learnt as a result of writing. Writing about an area we are a little unsure of may help us clarify our ideas and we may learn in the process of writing. By writing we may help other people to learn when they read what we have written. Results of this kind can be referred to as cognitive outcomes.

A third kind of result which we get from literacy has to do with its effect upon our emotions. We may get pleasure from reading, it may anger us or even make us afraid. It can also change or confirm our attitudes towards particular things. Writing can have similar effects. As we write we may develop our attitudes and feelings towards what we are writing about, or we may develop those things in the people who read our writing. Results of this kind are referred to as affective outcomes.

Literacy Involves Using a Range of Formats

You will have noticed from your analysis of your literacy events that you were having to deal with a range of formats in both reading and writing. Spend some time now listing the formats you dealt with and then see if you can add to this list. Compare your list with the list below, which is not intended to be comprehensive.

books	brochures
stories	advertisements
poems	pamphlets
newspapers	forms
letters	timetables
graphs	instructions
diagrams	maps
magazines	computer screens
notes	posters etc. etc.

What Are the Implications for Literacy in Schools?

In a sense the remainder of this book is an attempt to deal with the implications for the teaching of literacy in schools. In each chapter we shall set our discussion of the literacy environments and activities schools may provide into the context of the needs of the world outside schools. In this section we shall begin this process by discussing briefly some of the implications which arise from the four characteristics of adult literacy we have just presented.

Purpose

Most adult use of literacy is purposeful, as we discussed earlier. We pointed out then its two major types of purpose: the functional and the recreational. How does this fit with the experience of children in schools?

The first question here is simply, do children experience literacy in school as a purposeful activity? The answer appears to be that for many children the purposes for their engagement in literacy reside in their teachers' minds rather than in themselves. This is not to say that these engagements are purposeless, but merely that the purposes of them may be clear to the teachers but not to the children. This in itself is rather an odd state of affairs. We are not used, as adults, to reading and writing without knowing why we are doing these things. We may have been instructed to do them, but most adults will go further than this, and will not just take it on trust that the person who has given the instructions knows what is best for them. Yet this is precisely what children do in many of their school activities.

You might spend some time considering what might be done about this.

> Would it be desirable for teachers to ensure that their pupils always knew exactly why they were engaging in literacy activities?
>
> Is this simply a question of the teacher giving children a reason?
>
> Might it imply that the activities themselves are purposeful at the children's level as well as the teacher's?
>
> How feasible is this aim in the busy classroom situation?

The second question to arise from this consideration of purpose is, are the purposes adults have for engaging in literacy the same as children's? Children undoubtedly can use literacy for functional purposes, and for recreational, and we would hope that they get experience of doing this during their school careers, in preparation for the use of literacy in the world outside school. There is, however, another purpose which drives children's use of literacy in schools which barely concerns adults. This might be termed a developmental purpose, and simply involves reading and writing to get better at doing them. Children, of course, go to school to learn to use literacy, and a major purpose of the activities they take part in is to improve their mastery of the processes. This sounds unproblematic, but does give rise to some interesting questions which you might like to discuss.

> Does the developmental purpose for literacy activities conflict in any way with other purposes?
>
> Is it possible for the teacher to plan literacy activities for children in which both developmental and other purposes might be satisfied?
>
> Is it possible to involve the children in the planning of their own literacy activities?

Strategies

We listed earlier some of the strategies which experienced readers and writers use. The obvious question arising from this concerns the degree of experience and instruction in using this range of strategies which children commonly get in school. This experience will clearly be patchy, but there does seem to be a tendency to teach reading and writing as linear, single strategy activities. With reading a great deal of emphasis will inevitably be placed in the very beginning stages on word-by-word progression, and each word will be pronounced out loud. The effect of this may be to produce readers who only have that strategy at their disposal, and who do not easily develop the alternative strategies which they need. This effect will need counteracting at some point.

With writing a similar situation may develop. Teachers may treat writing as if it were uni-paced, and expect children to write steadily and evenly. Pausing too long between bouts of writing, and writing too fast to take care over letter formation will both tend to be disapproved of. Children may learn to try to avoid approaches in writing which, as we saw earlier, are actually normal and positive. Again this situation gives rise to some interesting questions which you may like to consider.

> How might children be taught to skim and scan as well as read intensively?
>
> How might they be shown how to switch between strategies in accordance with their purposes for reading?
>
> How might teachers build more flexibility into their pupils' approaches to writing?
>
> How early in a child's literacy learning is it possible to introduce a multi-strategic approach?

Outcomes

Children's use of literacy may well have a similar range of outcomes to that of adults. They may, through reading and writing, be moved to action, learn new facts and ideas, and respond emotionally. Sometimes, however, none of these outcomes may happen, and sometimes an outcome peculiar to learners may result.

No outcome at all is, sadly, more common as a result of children's literacy activities than we would wish it to be. All teachers will have met children who read pages out loud from their books, but seem to remember nothing of what they have read. A similar result happens with some children completing worksheets based upon their reading books. They do the activities, but learn and remember nothing, are inspired to little action, and the only effect on their attitudes may be a confirmation that reading and writing are 'boring'. With writing also, some children write only to regurgitate ideas they have been given, from which they learn little, and which certainly do not teach anybody else anything. This bleak picture is not, of course, universal, but the fact that it happens at all is worrying, and suggests the need for some thought about these issues.

Children's reading and writing in classrooms often has, in addition, an outcome which is not usually found in that of adults. This is that, for a great deal of it, somebody makes an evaluation of how they perform. Teachers constantly evaluate children's reading and writing, with the aim of helping them to improve it. This evaluation is not wrong in itself. It can be very useful and can lead to some well-aimed and effective teaching. The only slight doubt about it comes if we compare what happens to adult reading and writing. It is quite rare for someone else to evaluate this, but common for adults to evaluate their own use of literacy, from an awareness that they have not understood something they have read, to an assessment that their writing is badly phrased. This suggests that at some point teachers need to help children begin to evaluate their own literacy performance.

Several questions arise from these issues which again you might spend some time considering.

> How can we ensure that children's reading and writing has some practical outcomes which they can appreciate?

> How can we encourage children to evaluate their own performance in literacy activities?

> How can we move children away from over-dependence upon their teachers in their use of literacy in the classroom?

Formats

If we compare the wide range of formats which we have to learn to cope with as adults with the range children commonly meet, we immediately recognize a mismatch. Children tend to be limited in the range they use. In reading, the most common format will be the book, and in writing it will be narrative (stories). This is not to argue that there should not be a large presence of books in the school literacy environment, or that children's natural affinity with narrative should not find expression. The point we would like to make is simply that these should not be the *only* literacy formats children encounter, a point which will reoccur in the following chapter. You might at this point think about the following question.

How might we give children experience of reading and writing in an extended range of formats?

Summary

In this chapter we have tried to set the scene for the remainder of the book by examining the question of what literacy is and how it is used. We have touched upon some of the implications of these issues for the teaching of literacy, but much of the rest of the book will take up these implications in much greater detail.

We began with the observation that we live in a literate society. This being the case it seems logical that schools should prepare children to succeed in this society. They are, however, also societies in their own right, and one of the chief questions raised in this chapter is the degree to which the school environment can be made more reflective of that outside school in the presence and importance of literacy. The level of presence of literacy will convey important messages to children in school. In the following chapter we shall look more closely at what these messages might be.

Chapter 2

Looking at Literacy in Classrooms

A Classroom Cameo

It is 11.30 a.m. on a typical day in a fairly typical top infant classroom. As we examine this classroom in more detail we shall be concentrating particularly on the ways in which the classroom environment, the activities provided and the actual actions of the participants in this classroom may influence the beliefs the children come to hold about what literacy is and what it involves. It can be quite difficult to tease out the messages children get from particular elements of their experience of a classroom. Much of this analysis is speculative, and we may decide that children receive contradictory messages from different aspects of their classroom. But it can still be revealing to try to look at a classroom in this rather different way.

We shall concentrate first of all on the classroom itself. As we look for the first time think generally about the kinds of literacy experience provided for the children in this classroom. Do you think children in this classroom are likely to be encouraged to regard literacy activities as worthwhile and as enjoyable? What might the classroom be conveying to them about what literacy consists of? Make some notes about your reactions to these questions as you read, and compare them with our observations later in the chapter.

The Classroom

The classroom is reasonably spacious. Although it contains thirty children they are not obviously squashed together, and indeed there are parts of the classroom which are empty at the moment. The major furniture in the classroom is a series of rectangular and circular tables arranged in no obvious pattern in the middle of the room. One corner of the room has a rectangular piece of carpet on the floor, with several cushions scattered on it. There are also some chairs here, but no tables. On the walls in this corner are two low-level bookshelves, and a small book display rack. Books are attractively displayed in these, and on the top of the bookshelves there are some small potted plants and vases of flowers. On the walls above and around the shelves there is a display of children's written work and pictures, under the large caption 'Books We Like'.

Another corner of the room has been designated the class shop. A counter has been made from a table surrounded by painted corrugated cardboard, on which various home-made 'goods' are on display. These are labelled and have each been given a price. Pinned to the cardboard surround of the shop are various notices such as 'Buy your Mars bar here — only 8p', and 'Your local shop — use it or lose it'. Behind the counter is pinned a list of the goods for sale in the shop along with their prices. There is also a toy till and a supply of plastic coins.

A third corner of the room is arranged as a home corner and has wooden screens around it with windows and a door. Inside there is some toy furniture including a cooker, fridge, ironing board and also a cot with a doll inside.

The fourth corner of the room is occupied by the teacher's desk. This faces out into the room and on it are two piles of exercise books and a large dictionary. There is also a large notebook open in front of the teacher. On the wall behind the desk there is a small piece of pinboard on which are various notices such as a timetable, and other documents intended for the teacher's eyes, alongside a chart of all the children's names indicating the reading books they have read and are currently reading.

The walls of the classroom are attractively decorated with a variety of displays incorporating both teacher-produced and child-produced materials. In addition to the book display already mentioned there is a display captioned 'Ourselves' which consists largely of graphs of children's hair colours, eye colours, heights etc. There is also a display entitled 'The Iron Man' which consists of children's written work and pictures mounted around a three-dimensional robot made of cardboard boxes. Hanging from the ceiling in this part of the room are lots of small cardboard robots and bat-like creatures, intermingled with pieces of card on which are written words such as 'stupendous', 'horrendous', 'gigantic' etc.

Now let us look at what the children are doing in this classroom. Again you might like to make some notes about what you think they are picking up from the nature of their activities about literacy. Would you say these children are acting in ways similar to literate adults? If not, what differences do you think there are?

Children

Groups of children in the classroom are doing different activities. One group is working with maths workcards. Some of them are measuring each others' handspans, foot lengths etc. Two are sitting at their tables writing in their exercise books. Two more are using a set of balance pans and a jar full of beads to weigh objects such as books, shoes etc.

A second group is involved in a variety of activities in two corners of the classroom. Some of these are using the class shop. Two are behind the counter taking plastic money in exchange for home-made 'goods', while three more pretend to buy items from the shop. In the opposite corner of the classroom five children are using the book collection. Three boys are excitedly turning the pages of one book while pointing at various items and chattering animatedly. Another boy is lying full length on the carpet obviously engrossed in a book he has chosen. A girl is browsing among the collection of books on display, occasionally taking one down and looking at it more carefully.

A third group of four children is working together at a large table on a collage picture of a circus scene. There is a book on the table near them open at a picture of the circus. The children are talking together but do not actually seem to be looking at the book.

A fourth group is all sitting quietly at their tables writing on banda worksheets. There are at least five different worksheets being used by this group. Three of these children also have reading scheme books open on their tables. Only two of these children are talking to each other, and these two seem to be involved in an animated discussion about the worksheet they are doing together.

Now let us focus on the teacher. What do you think her activities as described here might be conveying to the children about the nature of literacy?

Literacy in Action

The Teacher

The teacher is sitting behind her desk, facing the class. A girl is standing alongside her reading from a book. Another child is asking her a question about his work. She diverts her attention from the child reading to answer the boy's question. The girl carries on reading. When the girl reaches the end of the page she is reading, the teacher tells her 'Well done', and the girl goes back to her place. The teacher writes something in her notebook, then calls another child to bring his reading book to her.

Analyzing the Cameo

Our main focus in this chapter is an examination of the messages the children in this classroom are getting about literacy. As we look at this we shall find that there are several points on which it is very difficult to judge, because we simply do not have enough information. It is equally as important for you to recognize these points as to make judgments on the basis of the information we do have. If you have made notes about your reactions to this classroom description, you might like to re-read them at this point to pick out points on which you feel you really need fuller information.

The Classroom

We shall begin by examining more closely the literacy environment in this classroom. What do you think this classroom environment is telling these children about what literacy involves and how important it is? Do you think the classroom reflects the full range of literacy as discussed in Chapter 1? Are there any ideas you think are insufficiently reflected? What alterations would you like to make to this classroom to reflect what you might consider a fuller view of literacy? Remembering the view we discussed earlier that literacy involves not just being able to do things, but also having some motivation to do them, do you think that this classroom is likely to encourage children in this positive attitude to literacy? Re-read the first section of the cameo, and spend some time thinking about these questions and noting down your ideas before reading any further. Our comments are intended not as complete answers, but rather as points to stimulate you to further thought.

Comments

(a) The first and most positive point to make is that reading is obviously valued and encouraged in this classroom. The attractive book corner and the display based on 'The Iron Man' are clearly designed to encourage reading and to interest the children in books and stories. The teacher has obviously taken care with this aspect, making the books look appealing, and making space for the children's reactions to them — which themselves are likely to encourage further reading. She has also used books to stimulate language development. Clearly a great deal of language usage has gone on in response to 'The Iron Man' and a deliberate attempt has been made to extend children's vocabulary, in this case by highlighting 'gigantic' words.

The chief message the children would seem to be getting from this environment is that reading is enjoyable and fun. This is entirely commendable and, of course, the kind of message we would like all classroom environments to convey. It is important, though, to recognize that this is not all there is to literacy. Think back to our discussion in the previous chapter. There we stressed that an important function of print in our world is to convey information, and the concept of literacy must include the ability to process this information. Does this classroom environment assist the children in any way to develop this aspect of literacy? Does it reflect at all the various ways print is used in the world outside school? Spend a few minutes now re-reading the description of this classroom looking for instances where print is used to convey information and reflect the print environment of the outside world. Look also for any missed opportunities where print could have been used in this way, but is not.

(b) You will almost certainly have pinpointed the class shop as a good example of the use of environmental print. Here print is being shown to the children to have a value in communicating information. Labels on the goods tell them what is for sale, and price tags tell them how much things cost. This is reinforced by a list of goods and prices displayed behind the counter. Print is also being used here in a way often neglected in classrooms, but everywhere seen in the outside world. Advertising and publicity notices form a major part of everybody's everyday print experience and they feature in this part of this classsroom. Of course, it is possible that some people might object to this feature on the grounds that children are exposed enough outside school to print trying to persuade them to do things, usually to spend money, without bringing this kind of print into the classroom as well. This is a problem, and we do not know enough about this classroom to know whether the teacher is alert to this and has done anything about it. Before reading on, think for a few minutes about how you might overcome this problem, and use advertising and publicity print in your classroom in a positive way.

(c) Clearly it is possible to do this in a big way by making advertising the theme for classroom work. A project on advertisements ought to have as a result an increase in children's critical appraisal of the publicity they see around them. However, there are two further suggestions we would make which operate in a smaller but perhaps more pervasive way. Firstly, it is likely that advertisements are at their most effective when they are perceived almost peripherally. They are designed to be glanced at rather than studied. If we do study them we tend to bring our critical faculties to bear on them much more readily. This suggests that in the classroom an effective way of stimulating children's critical thinking might be to actually discuss with them notices and signs as they are displayed, rather than simply allow them to become 'part of the wallpaper'. Of course, this discussion should include a healthy dose of scepticism on the part of the teacher.

The second suggestion is to consider who produces such publicity notices. Perhaps involving the children themselves in doing this might alert them to the kinds of techniques and 'tricks' they have to use to try to persuade people to do things, and thereby make them more critical of these technqiues when they see them.

Although environmental print is used to effect in the classroom shop, there are several other parts of the classroom in which the opportunity seems to have been missed. Take the book corner first. It seems a little strange that advertising notices are not used to worthwhile effect here. The major purpose of arranging the book corner in the way it is here is to persuade children to read, and notices such as 'Reading is good for you', 'You're never alone with a book' etc., would seem to have potential in furthering this message in a way which reflects the use of print that the children see outside school.

It is also a little odd that one of the chief places in this classroom where 'print for information' is used is not intended for the children at all. The teacher's notice board might provide a model for a wider use of this kind of print, and the development of the literacy necessary to use it. A class notice board, containing perhaps a timetable, a list of forthcoming events, a school dinner menu etc., and regularly updated by children and teacher, would seem to have a lot of potential here.

Perhaps the most glaring missed opportunity in this classroom is the home corner. It is unoccupied at the time of this description, and perhaps this indicates that the teacher does not attach too much importance to it, with a class which some people might consider too old to spend much time 'playing'. It is possible, however, that were it transformed into a 'literate' home corner, it might have more potential for developing positive attitudes towards literacy. At the moment reflections of the literacy environment provided by all homes are conspicuous by their absence in this home corner. Before reading on, see if you can jot down some of the things you think might be added to this home corner to make it reflect more accurately the print-rich environment in which children live at home.

(d) Imagination is the only limit here, but your list might have included such things as:

> Newspapers, magazines, TV and Radio Times
> Various pens and pencils
> Note-pads, letter-pads, envelopes
> A wipe-clean shopping list pad
> Recipe books
> Instructions for working the cooker, fridge, etc.
> Telephone directories
> Bills, final demands (!)
> Books for children to read themselves, and
> Books to read to the baby (doll).

All homes will have some of these things, and most will have them all. The home corner should really reflect this.

The effects of the omissions just detailed are mitigated by the positive use of environmental print in the class shop, but there is still a risk here that the children's attitudes towards literacy might be shaped in a way often seen in primary classrooms. Literacy as defined in schools, and literacy as defined in the outside world tend to be two different things, and there is a danger that children perceive them as entirely separate, and hence do not make the connections they should. For children in school, literacy is basically about books. At best, as in this example, it is about lots of varied and interesting books which they are encouraged to choose from and develop enthusiasms for. At worst, it is only about the reading scheme book they are told to read, two pages at a time, out loud to their teacher, every couple of days. For children outside school, literacy is about the many and varied ways print is used to give information, to persuade, to warn, to create and develop relationships, and, above all, to convey meaning. Separation of the two literacies in this way does not necessarily mean that children will fail to learn to cope with print in the everyday world. Most adults, in fact, manage quite well with most of it without being specifically taught. What it does mean, though, is that school may be seen as fairly irrelevant to real literacy, and the kinds of literacy it teaches as peripheral and very specialized to a particular environment. Elsewhere in this book you will find many suggestions for ways of linking literacy teaching in the school to the literacy experience children face, and will face, in the outside world. The first step, though, as always, is to look critically at your own and others' practice to determine where changes need to be made.

The Children's Activities

Our next step is to look more closely at what the children are doing in this classroom, and to attempt to analyze the effects these activities may have on their attitudes to literacy. Remembering our comments about the classroom environment, re-read the children section of the cameo, and make some brief notes about the kinds of messages about literacy you think are being conveyed to these children by the activities in which they are involved. Do these children seem positive towards the literacy activities they are doing? Are they involved in the full range of literacy activities? If there are areas less fully represented what effects might this be having? What about materials? Are these representative of the range of materials upon which children might exercise their literacy outside school?

Comments

The first point to make about the kinds of activities in which these children are involved is that the teacher's emphasis on encouraging them to enjoy reading books seems to be working well. The group in the book corner are obviously thoroughly enjoying themselves, and one would guess have been convinced that books offer them very worthwhile experiences. They also appear to recognize that reading can be an enjoyable *shared* experience. In fact, with the exception of one group, the children in this classroom seem quite prepared to cooperate and share their activities, and their use of their reading.

Most teachers would agree that this was beneficial for children. Yet it is interesting to note that, as in many classrooms, this cooperation does not seem to extend to reading and language work, where it might be expected to be of major benefit. The reason for this seems to be mostly attributable to the fact that the reading/language group here are following what is basically an individualized scheme of work. Such schemes, typified by reading scheme books linked to sets of worksheets, have become very popular in many schools during the last few years. Without doubt, one of the reasons for their popularity is the impression they give of providing a variety of activities matched to the needs of individual children. Hence the schemes are very often used as individualized systems, sometimes in direct contradiction to the advice given by their publishers on how they might be used. This, of course, militates against children discussing and sharing their work, and they begin to pick up the message that literacy activities in school are basically things you do by yourself. Notice that this does not happen as a result of anything the teacher might explicitly state about working together. From the way the rest of this classroom is organized it is likely that the teacher in this example is very receptive to the idea of children working together. It is, rather, a result of the way the reading and language activities themselves are organized. In later chapters we shall look more closely at alternative ways of organizing these activities to make it possible for cooperation to take place, but you might at this point like to spend a few moments thinking how you might do it.

There are examples in this classroom of children using print in a variety of subject areas. The major use of print seems, however, to be as a source of direction. Both the maths group and the language group are using the print on their worksheets as a guide to what they have to do. Nobody in the classroom is using print as a source of information. The group which might have been expected to do this most of all, the collage group, are, in fact, not consulting the book they have available at all. Perhaps the fact that there is a good picture there for them to look at is responsible for this, but it seems a golden opportunity has been missed here to show these children that reading information from a book can give them background knowledge with which to do other things. It is likely that the book they have in front of them has a description of a circus in addition to the picture and, had they been asked to base their collage on this description, they would have gained valuable experience of reading with real purpose. Again the encouragement of children to use print as a source of information seems lacking in this classroom.

Also missing in this classroom is any indication that the children use aids to learning other than the traditional school books and worksheets, although, of course, we do not know that such things as tape-recorders, video and computers are not used at other times in the school week. However, it does often seem that classrooms do not reflect the experiences of children in their homes, where they will probably be familiar with television, video, tape-recorders, record-players and even computers. These devices all have a valuable role to play in the development of literacy, which we shall investigate in more detail in later chapters. Our point at the moment, however, is simply that if classsrooms do not make use of these things then the message that school is somehow remote from the everyday world is being reinforced. This is a dangerous message which can result in school and the values and skills it attempts to pass on being seen as peripheral and, indeed, largely irrelevant to children's real lives.

The Teacher's Actions

The third source of influence upon the messages about literacy which children get in classrooms is what they see their teacher doing. Their teacher is obviously an important person to them, and what they see her doing can have a far greater influence upon their attitudes and behaviour than may often be realized. At this point you might like to re-read the very brief description in the cameo of the teacher's actions, and think about what messages she may be passing on to the children about literacy. Do you think there might be any kind of a gap between the messages this teacher is trying to convey by the way she has arranged and organized the classroom and the way she chooses to spend her time during this brief snapshot of classroom life?

Comments

(a) By any token the teacher in this example is clearly an excellent organizer. She has a well-ordered, stimulating classroom, and has developed the ability in her children to work purposefully, often cooperatively, on a varied range of interesting and worthwhile tasks. Because her system is working so well, she is able to spend time giving individual attention to the children in her class, and she has chosen to spend this time on a task highly valued by parents and most teachers alike: hearing children read aloud.

There are, however, two questions we need to ask about this. Firstly, while the teacher is hearing children read, she obviously cannot be doing anything else. She has, therefore, made the decision that hearing her children read is, at this moment, more valuable than anything else she could be doing. This is a question of values, to which there is no hard and fast answer, but would you agree with her decision? Before answering spend some time thinking about what the alternatives are. What else might this teacher have been doing?

(b) There is obviously a range of answers to this question. Assuming that we exclude activities which do not involve her working directly with children, there are several useful things she could have done with each of the groups in the classroom. The maths group and the shop group may have benefited from having somebody with whom to discuss their activities (assuming they did not lapse into simply answering the teacher's questions, which is a very common result of teacher intervention into small group activities).

Any of the children in the book corner could have gained extra insights into what they were reading by discussing it with a sympathetic adult. She could, of course, also have simply gone to the book corner and read a book herself, thus modelling the kind of behaviour she was trying to encourage in her children. The collage group could have been shown how to use the book they had as a source of information for their picture. The language group could have been encouraged to discuss with each other the work they were doing.

Of course, simply listing alternative things to do is not sufficient. Teachers always have a range of alternatives open to them, and they have to decide from moment to moment which to give their time to. Judging the respective values of these alternatives is not always easy. This brings us to our second question, which is to attempt to assess the effects of what this teacher actually does. How do you think it is likely to influence the views about literacy held by these children?

It is probable that, given a long enough exposure to this activity, the children will come to see this teacher, albeit subconsciously, as a custodian of literacy in this classroom. Although they will recognize the value she places upon reading for pleasure, if her actual time is spent mainly on hearing them read, the children are likely to consider this to be the thing she really thinks is important. By going to a special place to read, the activity itself becomes special. The place they go to is isolated from the rest of the classroom, by being *behind* the desk. It is of high status, since it is the teacher's place, and it is the control centre of literacy activities in the classroom. The presence on the teacher's desk of what seems to be the only dictionary confirms this. The teacher is the guardian of literacy. Most children come to place a high value on going to read to their teacher. This does not come about simply because of what one teacher does, but experience over several years tends to confirm this for children.

Now, if this activity comes to assume such major importance for children, and indeed for many becomes what reading is really all about, then it matters crucially what it actually consists of. And for many children, as is echoed in this example, what it seems to become is a very passive activity. The child has simply to say what is on the page. There is little incentive to derive meaning from what is there. The child is unlikely to be questioned about what it means. Indeed, the child will often be lucky to get the teacher's full attention. Distractions are common and teachers hardly ever give their undivided attention to readers for longer than a minute or so. The child may get the impression, then, that it does not really matter to anyone whether what she reads means anything. In fact, what will most likely matter far more is whether she can say it accurately. Teachers will often focus unduly on mistakes, without even realizing that they are doing it. If the child manages to get through her reading fairly accurately, she will be informed that she 'read well', and, reward given, return to her seat, confirmed in her impression of what her teacher defines as 'reading'.

In later chapters we shall consider alternatives to the practice of hearing children read, which might give children different impressions of what literacy involves.

Conclusion

What we have tried to do in this chapter is to look quite critically (you might think over-critically) at what is taking place in a classroom which most people would recognize as fairly typical. We have not been so much concerned with the outcomes of what is happening here in terms of the learning progress made by the children. We have no information on which to judge this, although we would expect this kind of classroom to produce quite good results in this way. What we have been examining is more subtle but, we would argue, more pervasive and more important in the long term. Everything that happens in classrooms influences children to some degree, and we have been examining the ways in which the environment and the events in this classroom might influence these children's views on what literacy involves. This we see as a crucial question, since it is clear that, for anyone, one's attitudes towards what one is doing are a major factor in one's success at doing it.

One of the most important functions of schools is to help develop literate children. In the previous chapter, we examined what is involved in this concept of literacy, and here we have attempted to tease out some of the, often very subtle, influences upon children's perceptions of what they are working towards. In future chapters we shall concentrate on examining possibilities for extending and developing literacy activities in the classroom.

Before reading further in this book, it would be very useful for you at this point to spend some time considering a classroom that you know well and trying to analyze it in a similar way to our analysis of this fictitious, but realistic classroom. You should be able to make a much fuller analysis as you will probably have access to much more detailed information that we were able to give you in a simple description.

Chapter 3

The Beginnings of Literacy

Language and Literacy Learning

Chapter 1 explained that literacy behaviour is both social and linguistic. Therefore any search for the origins of literate behaviour must begin by looking at language in its cultural context. Children are born into a social world: a world where people interact in numerous ways. As people interact they generate, and develop, values, attitudes and beliefs about the world and all the things in it. Language and literacy are two things within the world, but just as culture influences language and literacy, so language and literacy in turn influence culture. It is not a static relationship, nor is it a one-way relationship. Different groups in society develop different relationships to print and talk and these differences are manifested in the behaviour of both individuals and groups. Children born into cultural groups are inducted into the values, attitudes, and beliefs of that group, and that includes constructs about talk and print. Inevitably there are similarities as well as differences between groups.

A new-born child's first contact with the world is mainly physical. Its contacts with other people are dominated by closeness, comfort, warmth etc. However, thanks to those adults children are also surrounded by talk. Not simply talk between the adults but talk addressed to the child. Adults talk to children from the day they are born. From the moment a proud parent leans over and says 'My, you're beautiful, aren't you?' the child is treated as a fellow language user. Just as importantly as the talk to the child is adults listening to children and the sounds they make. In other words adults treat children from birth as communicating human beings. This has important implications for our understanding of how children develop as successful talkers and how they can develop understandings and knowledge about literacy.

In such communicative events the child's experience of language is holistic. Adults do not lean over prams saying 'a-a-a-a-a-a-b-b-b' etc. They use whole, meaningful chunks of language. The child does not experience instruction in how to talk. The child always hears talk about something. It rarely experiences talk taken out of context.

Suggestion for observation
Listen and, if possible, record a mother or father with a child under the age of one year. If possible listen or record without interfering in any way in the conversation.

Points to consider
— Do the adults talk to the child?
— Do they talk in reasonable whole language?
— Do they simplify their talk in any way?
— Does the child, in any way, join in with the conversation?
— Do the parents respond to the children's sounds as if they were meaningful and communicative?
— What was the talk about?
— What was the talk for?

An example
The short transcript below was recorded as a mother got her very young child out of a car and put it into a small pram.

Mother: Come on,
out we get,
lean forward a bit,
that's it, now this one.

Child: [Smiles and makes babbling sound]
Mother: You're happy today aren't you
[strokes baby's chin]
come on then,
that wasn't too bad was it?

Comments

The mother while physically moving the child does not ignore it verbally. All the action is accompanied by speech. It is speech that contains whole and complex utterances. The talk is directed to the child and accompanies particular types of movements. The child does not make a lot of sounds but when it does the mother responds both by action and through conversation. The mother is treating the child as a language user.

The above example is fairly typical when a child is alert and awake. If a child is to join the club of language users (Smith, 1988) it must work out how this object called language works. The drive to conquer language is the drive to assign meaning to events in the world. It is highly unlikely that children learn language to become linguists. They learn language because it is through language that they can explain, demand, organize, comment, and relate. By being 'meaning makers' (Wells, 1987) children's learning of language somehow takes care of itself. That is not to imply that children do not work hard at developing their knowledge of how language works; they do. However, the effort is purposeful effort; it is guided towards the realization of full participation in human society.

Children get a great deal of help from adults who create conditions which maximize the child's chances of becoming a fluent language user. It is important to note that it is good conditions that are provided not instruction. Parents very rarely instruct their children where language is concerned. When they do it is usually a very narrow point that is being made.

Adults provide a number of important conditions. They

— provide access to an environment where talk has high status;
— provide access to competent users of language;
— provide opportunities to engage in talk;
— provide responses which acknowledge the child as a competent user of language.

These conditions are fairly constant through the early years of childhood. In creating those conditions adults are welcoming children to the 'club' of language users.

Given such conditions it is not surprising that competence with oral language is achieved very early in life. And it really is competence. By the age of entry to formal schooling children will have achieved a considerable degree of skill in using the sounds of the language, in organizing the structure of language, in generating meanings with language, and in being aware of the subtle ways we modify language use for particular situations. Some children will be skilled in more than one language and a few in more than two. There is also considerable fluency. Children of 1, 2, 3, 4, and 5, have been recorded as using as many as 30,000 words in a twelve-hour period (Wagner in Crystal, 1986). They may well hear as many, if not more, words each day.

Children's ability to generate understandings about language is not unique. Indeed they are able to make sense of language because children are good at making sense of anything. Underpinning the drive to learn language is the drive to make experience meaningful; all experience. Children are active enquirers after meaning. They experience, reflect on that experience, attempt to account for it by generating beliefs, act, and consider the consequences for their beliefs. The work of psychologists such as Piaget, Bruner, and Donaldson reveal children who are actively constructing ideas to account for what they observe and experience. Young children, on the whole, expect the world to make sense and will go to great lengths to relate and order events, and to account for the phenomena they experience.

Suggestion for observation
Find a quiet time with a 3 or 4-year-old child. (You will also need a moment when the child is prepared to be publicly reflective and when it is not more interested in other things. It helps to carry out this activity with a child that you know fairly well who is comfortable in your presence.) Ask the child some apparently bizarre questions. For instance, 'Is milk bigger than water?' or 'Is red heavier than yellow?' (For further information about these and other questions asked of 5 and 7-year-olds see Hughes and Grieve, 1983.)

Points to consider
   — Do the children simply respond yes or no?
   — Do they bring other information to the answer?
   — Do they try to contextualize the question?
   — Do the children look at you as if you are stupid?
   — Do the children say the question is silly?

An example
Some questions were asked of 3-year-olds in a nursery school who were familiar with the questioner.

   Q: Is milk bigger than water?

Child: Yes.
Q: Why is it?
Child: Well, if you got — a big lot of milk, it's in a
     bottle — it's big and heavy —isn't it!

Comments

The child did not give the slightest hint that it thought the question
a stupid one (although some other children said that they did not
know, which might reflect a perception of an unanswerable question).
This child seemed to make sense of the question by bringing in a
context which allowed it to treat it sensibly. He related it to aspects
of his known experience which had to do with milk being in large
containers. It is probably more likely that most children will see milk
in large containers rather than water. The child treated the question
not as something totally confusing but as a serious event which
merited an answer grounded in reality.

The above observations suggest that children expect adults to make
sense. Perhaps, as Hughes and Grieve (1983) point out, children's
inexperience leads them to treat few inferences or explanations as
implausible. They treat everything as having meaning potential until
the contrary can be shown.

   If children bring meaning potential to events and objects then
what sense do they make of the experience of written language? To
what extent do they experience print within the same kind of
conditions that they experience oral language? To what extent is their
experience of print holistic and meaningful? In order to answer
these questions it will be useful to consider whether children's
experience with print occurs under the same kind of conditions as
their experience of oral language. Do the adults around a child offer
it access to an environment where print has high status, access to
competent users of language, access to opportunities to engage in
literacy, and do adults respond to children as competent users of print?

Do Children have Access to an Environment where Print has High Status?

The status of a phenomenon such as print should be judged by considering the frequency of occurrence, and frequency and type of use, rather than by what is said about it. There can surely be little doubt that for all children growing up in a Western environment print is a highly visible fact of life. Where does one go to escape print? Can one escape print? Even in the remotest places we carry it around with us and the by-products of other people's use of print are usually only too evident. As Chapter 1 demonstrated print pervades existence in a society such as ours. Print is a highly visible product on children, within homes, and out in the immediate environment.

Young children wear so much print. Apart from the labels that identify their clothes, their T-shirts, jumpers and jackets frequently feature the names of heroes and heroines, TV characters, and other objects.

Within most, if not all homes, there is a constant exposure to print. It is there whether we want it or not. It pours through doors in the form of free newspapers, circulars, political leaflets, letters and notices. All parents will, whether they want it or not, receive written material from their children's schools. Most print gets thrown out. It is a serious mistake to think of print as a static phenomenon. Only a small portion of the print with which we come into contact is ever kept for any length of time. Children's experience of print is often of it as a fairly transitory phenomenon, particularly if there are few books in a home. If there are books in a home and stories are read to young children then the status of print and print-related materials is considerably enhanced.

Print that is kept is usually kept for a purpose. It helps memory, keeps track of events, enables forward planning and generally helps organize lives.

Outside of the home print is saturating. It controls us, makes demands on us, extends invitations and offers, entices us, informs us, warns us, and generally embeds itself in our lives. It is extremely difficult to avoid its influence. Even adult illiterates develop strategies for making use of print. They may not be able to read it but they know it has function and significance. For most of us print in the environment is continually interweaving with our lives. It tells us what we need to purchase, when to buy, where the shops are, when the shops are open, how much items are, where the goods are in the shops, where to pay and what to pay with, which bus to catch to the shops, where to catch it and so on.

Children are witnesses to the existence of this print. Its quantity and pervasiveness let them know that it is something which people take seriously. However, its physical presence is given major significance by the use adults and older children make of it.

Do Children have Access to Competent Users of Print?

There will inevitably be considerable differences in the uses and extent of use made by adults of print. There will also be considerable differences in the extent to which adults allow children to be witnesses to their uses of print. However, the amount of use made of print is so considerable that most children will have access to extensive demonstrations of how print works, when it is used, what it is used for, where it is used and which print is used. It is the 'how', 'when', 'what', 'where' and 'which' demonstrations that really get children on the inside of the nature and purpose of print.

Adults' demonstrations of print use are not usually instructional (although they may be on purpose sometimes). They occur as adults use print for their own purposes. As they do so they provide multi-layered and multi-faceted demonstrations of print. When adults open letters and read them aloud, when they compose shopping lists, when they search for items in supermarkets, when they check a bill, when they read a newspaper, when they check the time of their TV programme, and many other events, they are providing a source of data about the way literacy functions.

In literate homes (and most homes are literate, even though they may use literacy in different ways and attach different values to it — Heath, 1983) such demonstrations occur frequently. Children will not always attend to them and when they do the attention may be very selective. However, they occur in such quantities in most homes that over a period of time the child develops its own hypotheses about this object called print or written language and begins to offer evidence of this learning.

Suggestion for observation
Find a time when you can sit quietly with a 3 or 4-year-old child. Have available paper and various forms of writing instruments. Start to write a letter, and allow the child to have free access to the materials. If the child does not respond tell the child you are writing a letter and ask it if it would like to write a letter too. (NB Clearly children are not always going to take up the opportunity. They may

at that moment be more interested in other things. If you are unlucky try again.)

Points to consider
Did the child ask what you are doing?
Did it write spontaneously?
Did it comment on what it was writing?
Did it use any technical vocabulary while writing?
What kind of marks did the child make?
Was the child able to tell you what it had written?

An example
The writing below was made by a 3-year-old child in such a situation as discussed above.

Example 1

Comments

During the session the child when told what the adult was doing spontaneously started to make marks. When the child was asked what it was doing it replied, 'writing a letter for mummy'. The child was able to use appropriately the term 'letter' and appreciated that letters were for someone. Its marks, although not involving letter-like shapes, have horizontality and appropriate verticality. The child was able to respond with a text for the letter. This child certainly understood certain features of written language and understood some aspects of the context of use of letters.

Some types of interaction offer optimal demonstrations relating to literacy. One such type is sharing books. Through sharing books children can be initiated into the emotional pleasures of hearing stories and the physical pleasures of the closeness which usually accompanies home reading. However, book sharing offers demonstrations of many kinds. There are demonstrations to do with the use of books (how we hold a book, where we start, the order of reading, the turning of pages), the vocabulary of books (front, back, cover, picture, print, author, story), and the readability of text (that the print gives the words of the story, we read it — usually — across the page, that print is made up of letters and words).

But beyond these technical demonstrations are those which contextualize books within lifestyles. There are demonstrations of how text can manoeuvre events, allow imaginative exploration, allow legitimate departures from truth, and can relate to personal experience. There are demonstrations of how text works, how narrative allows different ways of telling, how storytellers can switch roles and how stories start, develop, and conclude. The situations in which books are read provide opportunities for reflecting upon the content of books, the meanings of stories, and the relationship of the incidents and events to everyday lives and knowledge.

Suggestion for observation
Observe and, if possible, record a parent and a young child sharing a book.

Points to consider
How does the child respond to the story?
What kinds of questions does the child ask?
What kinds of questions does the parent ask?
Does the parent expand on any aspects of the story?
Does the adult refer to any of the technical aspects of book reading?
Who controls the pace and direction of the session?
Do either the parent or child relate any aspect of the text to real life?

An example

This extract is taken from *The Meaning Makers* by Gordon Wells, page 153.

Mother: [Continuing to read]:
        They chased the farmers from their hay
        They stung Lord Swell (chuckles) *on his fat bald* —

David: Pate.

Mother: D'you know what a pate is?

David: What?

Mother: What d'you think it is?

David: Hair.

Mother: Well — yes. It's where his hair should be. It's his head — look his bald head. All his hair's gone.

David: Where is it?

Mother: Well, he's old, so it's dropped out. He's gone bald.

David: Where's — Is that his hat?

Mother: Mn. He's running, so his hat's fallen off. (reads)
        They dived . and hummed . and buzzed . and ate.

Comments

In this short extract David, who is 3, is given a chance to explore some of the meanings within the book. Such diversions between readings are not uncommon and are one way in which parents help children develop a critical stance towards books. The message is that books are not just things to be read but objects to be commented upon and explored. The book, in this extract, is serving as a scaffold to allow the child to investigate concepts and ideas, and develop his understanding of both book-like adventures and phenomena of the real world.

Positive demonstrations of the nature and purpose of literacy are not on offer to every child and it is very important to remember that demonstrations can also be negative. If parents never read books or newspapers and never write letters, or instantly dispose of any print that comes into a home then the messages for children may well be that print is not a particularly useful element of life. Very few parents will never read or write anything but the quality and the quantity of the experiences will certainly vary considerably for different children.

Do Children have Access to Opportunities for Engagement in Literacy?

In homes where children are provided with books and where there are resources such as papers and pencils, children do not wait for opportunities to act in literate ways; they make them happen. Many parents will have experienced the attempts to pick up a newspaper or magazine when a young child is around. The adult reading seems to act as an irresistible lure to children who instantly demand that they are read to. In so many homes pieces of paper are thrown away by parents when clearing up after young children. Many contain marks intended as writing, written for a moment that is enjoyed and then forgotten.

In a recent survey of 400 parents of pre-school and reception class children (Hall *et al*, 1989) the majority of the parents claimed that they provided their children with free access to paper and materials which could be used for writing. Quite a few parents either allowed children to use the parent's desks or provided desks for the children's own use. Several young children identified by one of the authors of this book as having an early and developed interest in writing had been given their own desk or desk equivalent very early in their lives.

Children, through the ways in which they create opportunities for using literacy, are showing some of their understanding of the form and function of literacy. They 'write' letters and shopping lists, they make 'books', they 'write' stories, they create signs, and they use books extensively. In doing so they explore the forms which written language and written language use takes. Growing control over the forms in turn allows them to make more sense of the print environment. As this is noticed so it influences their marks. Thus in generating opportunities for literate behaviour a reciprocal process is maintained and literacy development takes place.

Do Adults Respond to Children as Competent Users of Written Language?

In many circumstances parents respond to their children's efforts in the spirit in which they occur. When a parent arrives home and is handed a torn piece of paper by a 3-year-old and is told that it is a letter, the response is usually pleasurable and enjoyable. The game often continues with the parent saying, 'What does it say?' or 'Why don't you read it to me?'. Equally when a 3-year-old sits with a favourite picture book and tells the story as it turns the pages, parents are often amused and continue with the game saying 'Will you read it to me now?'. So long as the behaviour is clearly identified as 'play' or 'pretend' then parents will accept what is offered, in much the same way as they accept bits of plasticine offered as buns.

However, parents' attitudes often change dramatically when the behaviour changes from being perceived as play and is viewed as 'learning'. With that shift comes a demand for fixed rigid behaviours. Accuracy becomes paramount and children's inventions will no longer do. It is often with literacy that formal instruction by parents begins.

As was pointed out earlier in this section parents rarely instruct in oral language learning. On those occasions when it happens it usually involves a mispronunciation or a mistake in identity. Even so correction and instruction form a minute amount of a child's experience of oral language learning. Parents tolerate children's attempts to communicate and the errors which occur as children develop hypotheses about the way in which oral language works. Why is it that parents respond so differently when written language is concerned? There are probably a number of reasons.

1 Oral language occurs in such vast quantities that life would become impossible if parents were to correct everything. For parents the concern is usually on doing whatever it is they are doing rather than on the language that is happening. For parents and for children oral language has a kind of transparency. We look through it to the meanings of the language because it is the meanings which are concerned with getting things done.
2 Parents are themselves the receivers of induction into social and educational systems. They were probably taught during the early stages of literacy learning through methods which stressed neatness and accuracy above meaning. Thus the model available to the parents influences their own interpretations about what counts as appropriate literacy learning behaviour for their children.
3 Correctness and accuracy are seen as necessary for success in schooling and later in life for earning a living. Possession of such knowledge is perceived as a form of power. Thus it is seen as appropriate that children get it 'right' from the start or, it is

believed, they will never be able to achieve their full potential and compete with others in the world.

4 It seems much easier to recognize and acknowledge 'correctness' in written language than it is to find it in oral language. This is because most written language that we see is printed. Thus newspapers, books, magazines, leaflets etc appear to offer a model of what correct and neat written language is. This correctness is however only apparent except in matters of spelling (and sometimes not even in that) as there are considerable differences in styles and usage among such media.

None of these is without some validity but with such a view of early literacy learning comes a number of penalties. The adults' model of correctness may override the child's previously successful learning strategies, the potential for generating confusion becomes considerably increased, and the child's natural inclination to investigate, explore and experiment in its learning is likely to be replaced by a demand to be told what to do all the time as well as refusals to undertake any learning which demands initiative.

It appears that in respect of the final condition there are critical differences between oral language learning and written language learning so long as the literacy related behaviours are judged to be 'learning' and not 'play'.

Conclusion

In many respects a child's experience of literacy appears similar to its experience of oral language. Children do live in an environment where oral and written language have high status. They do live in an environment where adults offer many demonstrations of oral and written language use, and they do have opportunities to use both oral and written language. There are though, inevitably, some important differences.

1 Children experience greater quantities of oral language than written language. It is also more immediate in that initially (apart from physical relationships) it is the primary link between the child and other people. This has three major implications. Firstly oral language will be learned before written language. Secondly it will not be immediately apparent to children what advantages written language has over oral language; after all oral language does pretty

well for the child's needs and concerns. Thirdly if a child's immediate environment is not a literate one then that child's interest in, and engagement in, literacy may be considerably delayed.

2 Many adults treat children's oral language learning as fundamentally different from children's literacy learning. So long as the literacy learning is just 'play' it is alright to respond within the definitions of the play routine. However, as soon as it appears to be 'real' then parents tend to demand a level of accuracy that was never demanded when children were learning oral language. The consequence of this is that children come to see the two activities as having a very different status. Learning oral language is somehow 'natural' and easy, while learning literacy is seen as a response to specific instruction and difficult.

The evidence, though, is now very compelling that given good literate conditions children do begin to put together the pieces of the written language puzzle in very similar ways to the manner in which they became orate. Within such environments they construct their theories of how written language works.

The Young Child's Construction of Literacy

In this section we will look in more detail at the beliefs that young children develop about literacy. It is important to realize that the examples given in this chapter may not occur for all children, may appear at very different times in a child's development, and, anyway, may not be manifested in a way that makes them known to adult observers. Children's beliefs can, of course, only be inferred; we cannot see inside children's minds any more than they can see into ours. Indeed it is the inner nature of much literacy behaviour (ie thinking) that makes it most unlikely that children will view literacy in the same way as competent literate adults.

When children watch someone writing or reading what are they to make of what is going on? What exactly do they see? They will see someone holding an object in front of their face and looking at it, or saying some words when they look at it. In the case of writing they will see someone taking a piece of paper and then using a pen or pencil to make marks on the paper. What the children cannot see is the process in the reader's or writer's mind; the all-essential process of interpretation or composition.

It should not, therefore, be surprising that young children do not make the same kind of sense of literate phenomena as adults. One way of examining this is to ask young children whether animals can read or write (Hall, 1988). Nursery-aged children are highly likely to laugh at the question. Despite many fictional animals which appear to read and write (Old Mother Hubbard's dog for instance) young children are fairly adamant that it is impossible. But why? The answer it seems is:

They ain't got no arms.

or

They can't talk.

or as one, more expansive child said:

Animals can't read and write because cats go 'miaow' and dogs go 'bow wow'.

The child's reasoning is easily explained by reference to its experience of reading and writing. It is something people do with their hands or/and their voices. Therefore it makes perfect sense to say that animals cannot read and write because they cannot talk or they haven't got hands. However, it is important to go beyond this aspect and ask how, given the somewhat internal nature of literacy processes, children move towards a more complete understanding of how literacy functions.

There are two interesting perspectives on how this happens. We will examine both and then consider the relationship between them.

A Psychological Perspective

The first perspective is a strictly psychological one. It is that of Ferreiro and Teberosky (1983). Ferreiro and Teberosky are Piagetian psychologists. When they look at children they ask themselves 'What kind of sense are children making of literacy?' They are not concerned with whether the children's views are right or wrong; they are interested in the beliefs, the constructs and concepts that the children are developing. For Ferreiro and Teberosky print is an object of knowledge just like any other object or set of objects in the world. Just as children develop knowledge hypotheses about how things move, why some things fall to the ground, why some things float, why people get angry, so they generate ideas about how print works.

Children will do this whatever they are told by adults. Anything they are told can only be interpreted by children in the light of the constructs they already possess. We are often surprised by the ways in which children interpret what we say or do. However, their behaviour, as indicated in the first section of this chapter, is usually the result of an attempt to make what we say or do make sense in their own terms.

Ferreiro and Teberosky have carried out a long set of studies into the ways in which children's ideas about print develop as they get older. They suggest that there is a sequence of stages through which children will go in their active construction of knowledge about print.

Their first level is one in which children search for an understanding of the difference between drawing and written language. From early in their lives children will make marks on paper and will perceive the activity as 'drawing'. However, they become aware that certain kinds of mark-making are regarded as different. Therefore the question children have to resolve is 'how?' It appears that early on children recognize two criteria for explaining the difference. One is that the lines of writing are arbitrary; that is they do not reproduce the shape or form of an object. In other words 'dog' does not have to look like a dog, whereas the drawing does. The second criteria is that written language is linearly organized. Thus when attempting to produce their own writing children will treat writing using these two criteria (see Example 2). When 'writing' at this level children frequently incorporate 'letters' into their writing. However, at this stage they are little more than random borrowings from the world of print around them. Children do not need to invent letters when they exist around them.

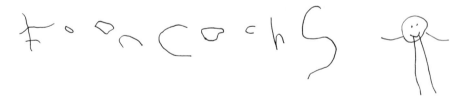

Example 2

One problem for children is, while recognizing that drawing and writing are different, to understand what the writing is for. Their hypothesis according to Ferreiro and Teberosky is that the letters or 'writing' somehow stand for the object.

However, it is not until children begin to move into second stage that they begin to sort out in what way the 'writing' stands for the object. They begin to answer this problem by believing that 'writing' stands for the name of the object. Children might, at this point, be learning to write their name, either at home or at school, so that type of activity may well influence their current hypothesis.

Once such an explanation is accepted it generates a further problem. If writing stands for a name, and objects have different names, how are those differences manifested in the writing? The main characteristic of this second level is the search for consistent reasons to differentiate between different pieces of writing.

At the first level any writing-like marks could stand for any name, label or text. During this second level children become increasingly aware that different objects need different types of marks. But what criteria are there for deciding which marks accompany which objects? Children start looking for those conditions which writing needs in order that it is readable (in the loosest sense of readable).

One principle identified by Ferreiro and Teberosky is 'the principle of minimum quantity'. Children in their studies said that something with only one letter could not be read. It was not until there were three letters present that all the children said that the writing could be read. However, this criteria is clearly not sufficient; there needs to be a way of discriminating between meanings. Thus children begin to demand that those letters have graphic variation.

One type of variation is to have different numbers of letters; they will observe that print can be long or short. They justify these differences by arguing that big objects have large numbers of letters. Thus 'elephant' has a long word, and 'ant' has a small word. Another type of variation is to change the types of letters used. Then the words can be the same length but can mean different things.

This is typically the level at which children use letter strings to represent speech or labels (see Example 3).

However, at this level there is still no understanding that the sound of the letter might have a relationship with what is actually written. This is the primary achievement of the last level. During this last level children have to learn and unlearn certain information. The first part is that children begin to account for differences by reference to the sound the letters, or the letter names, make. This is the stage at which invented, or temporary, spelling becomes readable providing one is able to get on the inside of the sound system the child is using (see Example 4a). In Example 4a, a 4-year-old has attempted to write 'Punch and Judy Show'. At first inspection it is difficult to make out

Example 3

what she has done. One of us watched the child write this and it was clear from observing that she had a clear concept of word. Although there are no spaces between words in the final copy the girl worked one word at a time. In Example 4b the words have been teased apart. Then is becomes clear that there is evidence of sound/symbol correspondence. 'Punch' starts with a 'p' and finishes with an 'e'. If you are wondering about the 'e' sound say 'punch' to yourself very slowly, just as a child would if trying to sound out a word. The second word is marked by 'a' for 'and'. 'Judy' begins appropriately with a 'd' sound and ends with an 'i' sound. She clearly has problems with the word 'show' but there is the use of the 'w's which must be related as they do not occur by accident in any of the other words. This child has a lot to learn but nevertheless understands that connections have to be made between the sounds and the symbol, and has begun to try out her theories about how print works.

Children at this level can be fluent writers. Indeed, if you can generate a reasoned spelling of a word then anything can be written. You do not have to queue up to get spellings, you do not have to avoid writing something because you cannot spell it; you can be an author. Children at this level demonstrate very clearly that they have little trouble discriminating between sounds. Indeed they are often better at it than adults whose ability to judge sounds has been corrupted by their having learned to spell conventionally.

As children's experience with text grows (particularly their experience as readers) so they will become increasingly aware that some, indeed many words, are not spelled as they sound. Thus starts the unlearning. Children now have to learn that rules operate in spelling that have nothing to do with the sound value of letters. It is at this point that one sees children misapplying the rules of spelling, but at the same time showing that they are aware that new rules apply. Of course for children growing up in countries where the writing system is very consistent with the sound values of the letters then such problems will be considerably less. However, for children in English speaking countries, many centuries of absorption of words from other languages, and other historical changes, demand that the irregularity of spelling has to be faced.

Central to the argument of Ferreiro and Teberosky is the notion that even though the hypotheses that children generate about language may be, in a conventional sense, wrong, they are, nevertheless, intelligent, reflective, behaviours. The children's hypotheses lead to problems which are profound ones to do with the nature of how literacy works. It is only because we, as adults, have left these poqeq doei lwqowíl

Example 4a

poqe   Punch

q   and

doei l   Judy

wqowíl   show

Example 4b

56

problems so far behind us that we fail to recognize them as fundamental problems of literacy knowledge. Children, when they generate these beliefs, are acting in a highly intelligent and efficient way. It would be wholly inappropriate to demean the ideas of children about literacy. On the contrary they should be recognized for what they are — sensible, and reasoned solutions to complex problems.

A Social Psychological Perspective

The second perspective starts with a stance which derives from psychology, sociology and linguistics. Harste, Woodward and Burke (1984) carried out a long series of studies into young children's literate behaviour. Whereas Ferreiro and Teberosky were interested in how young children saw literacy as an object of knowledge, Harste, Woodward and Burke were concerned with how children saw literacy as a process.

They were concerned with literacy in a much wider sense than Ferreiro and Teberosky. While Ferreiro and Teberosky were concerned about how young children understand the internal mechanisms of print, Harste, Woodward and Burke were much more concerned about how children understand literacy in a social sense; in other words not just how print works, but the where, what, why, and when of literacy in all its manifestations. Ferreiro and Teberosky see written language as a system to be known. Harste, Woodward and Burke see language as a way of mediating the world. Ferreiro and Teberosky would see literacy as the knowing of the system, while Harste, Woodward and Burke would see knowing the system as a consequence of literacy.

Harste, Woodward and Burke argue strongly that children are strategic in the way they approach learning in general and in particular the learning of literacy. They are strategic in that they use knowledge from a variety of sources to orchestrate what seems to be an effective response to any problem. Even their notion of what counts as a problem is strategic. Children analyze a situation using, again, a wide variety of knowledge sources, and it is the children who define, or do not define a situation as problematic.

Harste, Woodward and Burke argue that children bring to literate phenomena a complex set of strategies that derive from a number of sources. Some of these are linguistic, some are social, and some psychological. In their analysis of the children in their study they identified four main psycho/sociological strategies: negotiation, risk-taking, intentionality and fine tuning. These strategies are not strategies of childhood; they are the strategies of literate people. The principal claim of Harste, Woodward and Burke is that they found these strategies operating in very young children, who would not, conventionally, have been seen as knowing anything about literacy.

Unlike Ferreiro and Teberosky who see children as progressing almost inevitably through their levels, Harste, Woodward and Burke reject the idea that development in literacy follows a fixed sequence of stages. They would argue equally that development in literacy has nothing to do with IQ, class, colour or race. It has to do with experience, in particular experience in the freedom to negotiate, risk-take, fine tune and have intentions where literacy is concerned. They would argue that utilizing those strategies is learning, and that if children are inhibited from using those strategies then learning will slow down or cease.

The four strategies identified by Harste, Woodward and Burke must always be considered in the context of the overall response of a young child. Being strategic a child selects from a repertoire of choices. Thus any analysis of young children's literacy behaviour must involve looking at a whole range of events; the children's choices may be different for all of them. To a large degree it is the ability to make choices which marks out the effective user of literacy from the ineffective user. The child who cannot choose to vary strategies is stuck with a rigidity of response that may often be inappropriate.

What then, in practice, do the notions of Harste, Woodwood and Burke mean for our understanding of young children and literacy? If Example 5 is examined we see a relatively common product of the nursery school. A 4-year-old child has drawn a picture of herself and has written her name by the side of the picture. At least we assume that because no-one reading this book actually saw the order in which the components were put on the paper.

For Ferreiro and Teberosky the interest would be in the level of knowledge that this child has about the way the text is constructed. From their perspective it is remarkably uninformative. We might reasonably be able to assume that the child can differentiate between drawing and writing, but the fact that she has written her name does not tell us about the level of knowledge about the sound-symbol relationship.

Harste, Woodward and Burke would want to ask rather different questions about this piece of work. They would want to know about the context within which it was written. They would want to know what alternatives were available to the child. They would want to

Example 5

see the piece as a strategic response to the child's judgment of the context.

An example of strategy can be considered in relation to this piece. As one of us was present when this was carried out we can begin to analyze it. The piece was a voluntary piece in which the drawing was done first. However, the child has negotiated certain freedoms. This child has been taught to write its name by its parents and this was reinforced in nursery school. Katherine will never have been taught by anyone to write her name in sections thus the way she has chosen to represent her name here is either a mistake or a reasoned response to a judgment about the context.

As the drawing was done first the child was faced with a decision when after writing the first letters they butted up against the drawing. What does one do? Should the sanctity of name completeness and linearity be maintained and the boundary of the drawing be broken? Or should the drawing take precedence in which case previously learned behaviours relating the way in which one writes a name be disregarded? In this instance Katherine chooses to preserve the boundary of the drawing. To do this she may well have made a judgment that it is alright to break up the name so long as all the right letters are there. A child who could not be strategic would have had to write across its drawing, or reject it as unusable. Of course, as Katherine's experience of writing grows so she wil be able to predict such conflicts and may resolve them in advance by writing smaller or moving the location of the name (Hall, 1987b). Katherine's decisions show her willing to negotiate her freedoms, show a willingness to risk-take and a degree of fine tuning with language. Her intention of having a labelled drawing has been achieved without generating a mess of overlapping lines.

For all their differences both Ferreiro and Teberosky, and Harste, Woodward and Burke are concerned with analyzing the moves made by children. They are both concerned with knowing what it is that children do as they act in literate ways. They both believe that without an understanding of what children know about literacy, teaching strategies are little more than guesswork, and are likely to be inappropriate. Indeed both sets of researchers argue that conventional practices relating to literacy instruction take no account of what we now know about how young children learn literacy most efficiently. Ferreiro (1986) said:

> There are school practices that put the children outside the knowledge because they define the child as a passive expector

or as a mechanical receptor. In these kinds of settings children learn that all their questions are irrelevant. They learn to answer without thinking and to accept without resistance. (p. 10)

And Harste, Woodward and Burke (1984) say:

The reading and writing curriculum should not be isolated from other curricular areas but rather be a natural and functional part of the opportunities selected by the class for exploring their world. (p. 204)

Both sets of researchers seem to share some important assumptions about the implications of their work for children in nursery and other levels of schooling.

Ferreiro (1986) says:

Taking seriously the consequences of the psychogenetic development means putting the children with their assimilation schemes at the centre of the learning process (children that learn in social settings and not in isolation). It means accepting that everyone in the classroom is able to read and write (each one at his/her own level, including the teacher's level), understanding the developmental meaning of seemingly 'strange' answers (or questions), and acting in accordance with the problems children face at crucial points in their development. (p. 9)

and Harste, Woodward and Burke (1984) say:

Choice is an integral part of the language process. Participants in a language event have the right as responders, for example, to ask another question rather than answer the question asked, or as writers, to decide to allocate part of their text to art, context, inference etc. These rights need to be respected in the classroom. (p. 205)

Both sets of researchers acknowledge that in normal circumstances children do not sit passively waiting to be told what they should learn, but simply get on with learning by operating upon the world. They learn by having a go, by trying things out. Early childhood is a continual process of experimentation, risk-taking and negotiation, in purposeful, intentional ways. The task for schools is to allow that process to continue not stop it and replace it by imposed passivity. How that may be done is considered in the next section.

Looking at Literacy in the Nursery School

The previous sections have begun to illustrate certain very important points about the young child's developing knowledge of written language.

Amongst these points are:

That children have a powerful capacity for controlling their own learning, developing their own theories about written language, and acting strategically in the implementation of their beliefs.

That they do so with considerable help but little instruction from parents, and do so with little fear, or expectation, of failure; they expect to be able to do it and they expect their efforts to be taken seriously.

That being in a literate environment is a powerful aid to their learning, and that, in particular, being able to see adults use language and literacy in a wide variety of ways provides opportunities for reflection on the nature and purpose of written language.

The child's experience of language is of whole and purposeful language used appropriately for genuine reasons in social contexts.

As we move to consider children in nursery schools or classes it is important to ask whether such institutional environments acknowledge the significance of the above points for the continued development of understandings about the nature and purpose of literacy. Traditionally the literacy curriculum in nursery schools was (and in many schools still is) a kind of pre-literacy curriculum. It was concerned with discrete skills that were somehow supposed to cohere into readiness for formal instruction in literacy. Transferred into better known categories the skills were concerned with such elements as manipulation, articulation, audial-discrimination and visual discrimination. Few of these ever involved, in any complete sense, a literate act. The exception being story reading. In that type of curriculum the teacher was the informant; the child was simply the person 'told', and most of the 'readiness' activities effectively made sure that a child had an absolute minimum of contact with actual literacy.

The irony is that most nursery teachers believe that this time in a child's life should be set aside for the intellectual, emotional, and imaginative growth that comes not from systematic instruction but from the freedom to explore, and play with, a wide variety of materials and situations.

The kind of evidence already outlined in this chapter suggests strongly that the conventional 'sub-skills' curriculum is rather narrow and misguided. A more appropriate way of thinking about the literacy curriculum would be to see it as the provision of opportunities for children to engage in exploration, experimentation, risk-taking, generation, negotiation, modification and reflection under conditions much like the unofficial curriculum provided by parents for language development. That curriculum consisted of an environment full of talk, an environment full of talkers, and encouragement to engage at all times in meaningful communication. All that was accompanied by sympathetic support within a context of cooperative interaction.

Outside of school many children have been exposed to rich literacy environments. If such environments can be continued and developed within nursery schools then not only will those children be able to develop but those children whose experience has been more limited will be able to explore and learn about the nature and purpose of literacy.

An Environment which Demonstrates the Status of Literacy

The creation of a print rich environment with the appropriate provision of resources is a first stage in creating a school context for literacy development. A print environment will, inevitably, contain mostly material to be read, but as such it is also a demonstration of material which has been written. In order to develop as readers and writers children must have access to data about written language and written language forms; it is the print environment which provides much of this data.

If we want children to continue to explore through the making of marks and the act of reading the different uses of written material then children must have access to the print forms which adults read and use. Children cannot construct their knowledge of written language in a vacuum. Why shouldn't the library corner contain newspapers, comics, magazines, catalogues, timetables and posters? Children may not use them often and may not use them in the same way as adults but the items are nevertheless sources of information about written language.

Displays of 'print that we can read' or 'print that tells us something' will also provide opportunities for interesting children in the print data that surrounds them. It is amazing how much of such print gradually appears in their own mark making. It is unlikely to appear if the data is not there. While still dealing with written material it is important not to omit stories and other books. The importance of books and the ways in which children respond to them have already been highlighted in this chapter. The nursery school must continue to offer every facility for further exploration of books. Books should be read frequently to children and they should be discussed and evaluated. Children should have access to good books; they should have stories which make you care about the characters and what happens to them. There should be information books displayed both in the book corner and accompanying displays. All the books should be in good condition and should be displayed in ways which make them easily seen and easily used. There should be lots of books, and new ones should always be being introduced. Children who are becoming regular written mark makers love to make their own story books. They can have title pages, stories and illustrations. They may incorporate characters from stories they have heard and may wish to copy their names. The data collected from story reading gives form to the ways in which young children attempt to create their own written stories.

The wonderful thing about an environment which has interesting and varied displays of written material, is full of written material in use, and provides constant access to materials for creating print, is that it goes on working all the time. It is a constant physical demonstration of print as data, and, through your provision of materials, a further demonstration of your commitment to the importance of writing and reading.

Suggestion for observation
Spend some time in a nursery class examining and evaluating the status of literacy within the classroom environment. Concentrate on the physical manifestations of literacy (for further information about this see Hall, 1987, chapter 7).

Points to consider
— How much print is there in the room?
— How much of it has been generated by the children?
— What facilities and resources are there for writing?

— How are the books displayed?
— How many books are there?
— Is there any environmental print on display?
— How recent are any signs, notices and displays?

An example

An extract from a student teacher's initial observation report.

In the entrance to the nursery classroom there was a notice-board mainly for parents. It contained a number of recent notices and some samples of children's work, including some 'notices' made by the children. Just inside the door was a 'signing-in' sheet which was renewed each day. Each child 'signed-in' every day. Within the classroom everything was labelled; drawers had the names of their contents, areas had headings (and where appropriate, rules), and displays had accompanying descriptions and comments. All the children's work (and there was a lot of it) had the names of the children on it. The names had been written by the children. By a writing corner (which was supplied with a whole range of materials) was a notice board filled with the children's efforts at writing. A post box stood next to that. The book corner was well stocked and every book was displayed front on. In addition most of the displays had accompanying books. The displays also included children's writing. For instance the class had recently been growing seeds and every child had made a book recording what they had observed. These were standing by the growing seeds. Part of the work on the walls derived from a recent print-walk. It had a lot of environmental print, photographs of the print seen on the walk, and many copies of the print made by the children once they had returned to the classroom.

Comments

In this class the abundance of print provided a rich source of data for the children. There was also a considerable sense of involvement. Print was not just something done by teachers; it was something to which everyone could contribute. The print environment was a dynamic one. It reflected the real concerns of classroom life and, as a consequence, changed regularly. The children's efforts were valued and deemed worthy of display despite the fact that most of it was not in a conventional form. The environment supported growth in literacy by providing the children with a wide ranging view of the nature and variety of uses for print, and by valuing the children's efforts at being makers of literate marks.

An Environment with Literate People

A literate environment is a fairly meaningless concept without people who are using that environment; people who, through the variety of the ways in which they use print, demonstrate when it is used, how it is used, where it is used and what it is.

If you examine your own life as a literate person (as suggested in Chapter 1) you will be able to identify a whole range of literate behaviours in which you engage. You may keep diaries, write letters, write cheques, fill in forms, keep records, make lists, write recipes, take notes and read a multitude of different material. This list could be considerably extended and refined as it would have to include all those components which represent the life of a literate person in the Western print world.

But if teachers examine their literate lives as seen by the children in their classrooms then the richness often appears to dissolve leaving relatively few activities, and those that remain can usually be grouped as instructional activities. The children in a nursery classroom will see the teacher read stories, take a register, may see the teacher write captions for displays, and may experience the teacher's writing as caption making. But that may well be all! The potential of the world of literacy, and in particular of writing, is often obscured for children in nursery and infant classes.

Despite the poverty of the demonstrations children do make use of those that exist. A nursery teacher recently told one of the authors about a group of children playing school. They wanted to make a register and persuaded the teacher that they had to have her red and blue biros. And why not? They are, after all, the appropriate instruments if you are being a teacher.

Given the power of demonstrations to influence children's behaviour why do we not offer a greater range of demonstrations of literacy? One reason is a kind of fear of being found not teaching. Time and time again teachers report that they couldn't possibly sit there writing a letter or reading a newspaper. After all what would the head/adviser/parents say? Teachers should consider those fears in relation to the learning potential of the demonstration. If by providing a demonstration you are alerting a child to a purpose of writing and reading, helping it understand a form of writing, or revealing to a child how writing and reading work — then you are teaching! If, nevertheless a teacher feels too guilty about such behaviours then parents can supply such models in classrooms. Using parents to actually be readers and writers in classrooms has been relatively unexplored but is an area of immense potential.

Demonstrations of writing and reading should be an integral part of the literacy curriculum. They are a way of cooperatively exploring literacy within an interactive environment.

Suggestion for observation
Observe the behaviour of one adult, preferably either a teacher or nursery nurse, during one day at school. What kinds of literacy-related demonstrations are on offer to the children?

Points to consider
— What is the range of literacy-related activities engaged in by the adult?
— To what extent are they observable by the children?
— To what extent do they involve the children?
— Does the range of activities bear any relationship to the kinds of literacy-related activities adults engage in out of school?

An example
An extract from a student teacher's initial observation report.

During the day very few engagements with literacy were observed. It was only at lunch-time in the staff room that the teacher read a newspaper, looked at 'Child Education' and glanced at a catalogue. In the classroom the activities were almost always oral. The class had no writing corner and the nearest the teacher came to writing with the children was an activity in a work book involving dots to be joined up by the child drawing the lines. The teacher told me this was to help them be able to handwrite when they went to infant school. The teacher did not write names on the children's work and the children were not expected to write their own. Some displays had one word labels like 'Blue' accompanying a set of blue objects but both the display and the caption had been done after school. The only truly literate activity observed by the children was storyreading. The book was chosen by the teacher and no explanation was given for the choice beyond 'I thought we'd have this one today'. The book had been picked from a stock cupboard and was not one of the books on display in the library corner. I was told that they could look at those themselves. When I asked the teacher about writing and print in the classroom she told me that when she trained they had been told to avoid it as it was confusing for the children.

Comments

It will be very difficult for the children in this nursery class to develop, in school, any understanding of the usefulness or nature of most literacy activities. Even the story reading was an isolated event in which there was no involvement of the children in the selection of what was to be read. As far as these children were concerned literacy was not something in which adults engaged or something that adults found interesting or useful. The range of literacy-related activities observed by the children is extremely limited and when the print-starved nature of the environment is taken into account these children are clearly being given a very narrow and distorted demonstration of literacy.

It is important to explore, in nursery classrooms, ways of extending the richness of our demonstrations of literate behaviour. Children need data to form their judgments about the how, why, when, what and where of literacy. Perhaps part of the reason that so many children stop acting as 'critical enquirers after meaning' when they arrive in nursery school is that the teachers themselves, unlike parents, do not seem to do interesting things. They are too busy getting the children to take part in interesting activities.

Children will act as critical enquirers about literacy if they see the teacher using print. One nursery head that we know regularly takes her work and sits in a corner of the classroom. She does not actually get very much done. The children are constantly asking questions about what she is doing. She has made her work part of her literacy curriculum.

Teachers should attempt to make demonstrations of reading and writing part of their literacy curriculum. Can they list-make with the children, write letters to parents with the children, build up a well-used notice board with the children, write notes, write stories and poems, write notices and so on? Children will not, in any sense, become proficient, conventional readers and writers — but greater experience of the relevance and purposefulness of literacy will go a long way to help them appreciate the significance of print-related experience.

An Environment of Opportunity

Children need opportunities to experiment with and investigate all kinds of literacy operations. An environment which has extensive print materials on display and an attractive library area with plenty of good book provision will go a long way to helping children think about reading. It will also provide a resource for data about writing.

Writing is, in homes, a more context specific activity than reading. By this is meant that reading is something that can be done almost anytime, anywhere. Writing tends to be restricted to certain times and certain situations. It may well be the case that nursery schools can, in some ways, significantly increase the opportunities children have for writing. It will be clear by now that this does not mean by copying, tracing or handwriting exercises but opportunities involving genuine literacy acts. Children need opportunities to write as meaning makers. Those opportunities fall somewhat roughly into two categories: writing for writing's sake, and writing as a contextualized activity. They are not mutually exclusive classes.

It would be extremely rare for a nursery class to be without a permanent library corner where children can, when they choose, sit and look at books and generally act as readers. It ought to be equally rare for a nursery class to be without a permanent writing corner where children can, within minor limitations, choose to act as writers. This demands physical space and provision of resources as has already been indicated. However, children also need the freedom to use such an area, as far as possible, when and where they want, and most of all — how they want.

There is no place in the nursery school for restrictive controls on the use of mark making equipment on the basis that they will scribble everywhere if we just allow them general access to pencils and crayons. Children need free access to the widest possible range of materials and equipment. Do you write letters in crayon to friends? Children may decline to use certain forms because they do not have access to what they consider to be the appropriate materials. Let children have paper of different kinds, writing paper, envelopes of different sizes etc. Have low-level notice boards by these resources so that children can display their own work just how they want. Give the children some sense of ownership over their productions. Writing activities offer the children a chance to consider, and use, their print knowledge; print knowledge that has often been acquired from their reading activities.

Much of the writing that we do as adults relates closely to a specific function. We make shopping lists to guide us when shopping, we write in Christmas cards when it is Christmas, and we write notes when engaging in a phone conversation. By providing a variety of contexts within classrooms it is possible to supply opportunities to write for many different functions.

Structured play areas such as hospitals, shops, cafes, airports, garages, estate agents, offices, theatres, can frequently be found in nursery classes. However, it is much less frequent that reading and writing facilities are provided within those play activities. Yet why not, for in reality all those situations have literacy, often extensively, embedded within their boundaries. In the classroom these structured play settings should also, where possible, be accompanied by relevant printed or written resources. Children will use them eagerly.

Suggestion for observation
Find a classroom with a structured play area that does not have appropriate literacy-related material. Provide a range of such materials and observe the children's behaviour before and after the additions.

Points to consider
— What is the children's initial reaction to the new literacy provision?
— Do the children continue to use the new material as time goes by?
— Is the new material incorporated into existing play routines or does it engender new types of play?
— Do all the children use it in the same types of ways?
— To what extent do the children display appropriate use of the literacy-related material?

An example
This example is derived from Hall *et al* (1987).

A group of students took over the home-corner of a conventional nursery class. They had observed that the children hardly ever wrote and claimed that they did not know how. The students put in all the kinds of material that one would expect to see accompanying certain items in homes. Thus telephone directories, note pads and biros were placed by telephones. Recipe books, note pads and writing instruments were placed near the cooker. This 'home' was provided with a desk and all the associated resources. A newspaper was put into the area each day and letters were delivered each day. The home-corner was then videoed for one week. The children from the start made extensive use of the literacy materials and were very excited to see them there. During the week 290 literacy-related incidents were observed, many involving writing. The children both incorporated the material into their existing play routines and developed previously unseen areas of play (for instance, travel agent play).

Comments

The children working in this home-corner were now able to demonstrate a whole range of behaviours and sets of knowledge that had not previously been displayed. They demonstrated a commitment to literacy, substantial knowledge of the purposes of literacy, and were able to show that they possessed a range of understandings about the way literacy worked.

If children are given the opportunities to work with print then they have the chance not just to show that they know and can do, but to experiment and explore the types of literacy which are appropriate to those activities. Of course their use may often be unconventional but it will always be informative.

An Environment of Encouragement

Just as parents concentrated on responding to children as talkers so teachers must learn to respond to their children as literates. It is just about the most powerful form of encouragement that exists. It is the encouragement that constantly affirms a child's status as a legitimate user of print. Teachers must recognize children's efforts as emergent literates, be prepared to encourage them to explore written language, and discuss in a facilitative way the efforts the children make. Children also need praise for their efforts. Written language is a most complex phenomenon and success, at any level, with unravelling its complexities needs to be rewarded. It is however important that praise is linked with discussion, or there is a danger that children will cease to extend their exploration of written language. Such teaching demands sensitive teachers: teachers who are prepared to listen to, and watch, children; teachers who do not rush in to impose their own solutions upon the children; and teachers who respond to the particular concerns of the children while they are being readers and writers.

Conclusion

Access to print, demonstrations of written language use, and opportunities to use written language represent a curriculum of opportunity not a curriculum of control; a curriculum where the meanings of literacy and literate acts are cooperatively explored and developed within an interactive environment. In this curriculum the child and the teacher share the role of informant; both learn from each other. The sequence in the curriculum is negotiated by the child and the teacher. Each brings something to the encounter and each modifies their perspective as a result of the encounter. It is not a question of teachers just leaving children on their own in the hope that they will emerge as literates, but of teachers creating environments in which children can construct, realistically, images of themselves as genuine users of written language.

Chapter 4

Literacy in the Infant School

From Home to School

Whatever experience of literacy young children have within the home, the playgroup, nursery, in their community — they have all developed their spoken language to a remarkable degree. The accent and/or the dialect may not coincide with that of the teachers in the school — that is a difference not a deficit. The richness and diversity that this presents should be an asset in school, a language resource that can be tapped and used. Children's first language, their mother tongue, may not be English but you can be sure that it will be well developed and perfectly adequate for the child's needs and learning outside school — it is just the learning situation inside school that may at first present problems for the child.

Many children will have had experience of books, either being read to or perhaps even being able to read some books for themselves. Many children will be aware of print around them in their environment and they will know that this print carries a message and is not just a pattern.

Many children will come to school having had experience of writing. Parents and teachers may not recognize the marks on the page as letters and words but the child will be making marks with the intention of conveying a message. At this stage the 'writing' may be different on occasions, but the child has some important understandings about what writing is for and that it has a correspondence with talking.

Children have learnt a lot about language in the home and in the community before they come to school. They have not been formally 'taught' and they have 'learnt' by being part of a literate community, by using language in a social context.

Literacy in Action

Suggestion for observation and reflection
Think about the experience of very young children in the classroom
— list some ways in which you think the classroom situation might
be different from that of the home.

Points to consider
How often do children in the classroom have opportunities to talk
with adults?

How do you think the 'busyness' of a reception classroom might
affect children's talk?

Might the style of language spoken by the teacher to the child
be different from the style of language the child has been accustomed
to at home?

How can the classroom be made into a productive context for
children's developing literacy?

Comment

The pattern of activities at school is very different from that at home.
Schools vary tremendously in their rationale for learning and in their
organization of time and resources for the young child. The school
is an institution, though, and in every school there are set points in
the day for individual classes and for whole schools: dinner times
and arrival and departure times cannot be changed. Within this
framework, resources — materials and space — have to be used
effectively so there are set arrangements for these too.

In each individual classroom children are grouped together for
most of the day, either in informal friendship groups, larger teaching
groups or whole class groups. Essentially they are part of a much larger
community than that of the home and family. There is very little time
to relate to an adult individually as they do for most of the time at
home. Much of their learning must be from each other and through
the planned activities offered them. All this learning is either enabled
or enhanced through talk.

The research work of Gordon Wells in Bristol (Wells, 1987)
reflects the value of extended exchanges between caregiver and child
based in a familiar situation when the child and adult have a shared
knowledge of past and present events and a shared projection of
the future. It is very difficult for a classteacher to approach this
situation. Other adults present in the classroom with children can

help to provide situations for a sustained conversation on more 'equal' terms.

What of parents? They have been their child's 'teacher' up to now and children have learnt a vast amount about language from them. Has their role as 'educator' been entirely handed over to the teacher who may have over thirty children to whom she must be responsible?

In fact is it for social and economic reasons that we group children together at around five into a class within a school or can we justify this organization on educational grounds?

With questions about the social and the learning context in mind, let us look at the child in the infant school.

The young child's learning experiences in the infant school can be roughly divided into two categories: those which children choose for themselves and those which are directed by the teacher. The teacher may be present in the activities planned and organized by her or she may set up a context within which children will learn. In fact none of the activities that children choose to take part in are without influence from the teacher as everything that takes place in the classroom is derived from her thinking and planning.

Early in the morning session and in the afternoon session all the children will be together to listen to plans for the day. Whatever activity is planned by the teacher or initiated by the children, it is hard to imagine a context where literacy has no part. Every day there is at least one occasion when the focus is on reading or writing or talking and listening but all problem-solving situations involve talk, investigative situations are accompanied by talk and may be reflected on through reading and writing. Creative arts activities of painting, drawing, modelling, sculpting are accompanied by different kinds of talk for organization, comment, appreciation and reflection, affiliation, self-assertion, instruction.

Music and drama carry their own special form of literacy with songs, rhymes, chants, role play and improvization.

There are many times during the day in which children 'play'. The contexts for play are less teacher influenced than the contexts for 'learning'. There is, in fact, a false division implied in these two terms because children are learning continuously through 'play', the difference is that the learning in play is not so closely planned.

Children play with construction toys, jigsaws, word and letter games, counting and sorting games and with sand and water. They also 'play' in context specific situations like a home corner, hospital, dentist, bus stop, station and school. These contexts for 'play' are dominated by talk and within them children demonstrate their awareness of language register and appropriate talk as well as social relationship and differential status.

Focusing on Talk

From general considerations and questions about literacy in the infant school, let us now focus more closely on particular aspects of literacy. It is a truism to say that the development of literacy is a holistic process, with no one aspect developing in isolation. For the purposes of the next section of this chapter though, it is proposed to focus in turn on talk and listening, reading and then writing. These threads will then be woven together again in the last section of the chapter to consider the whole climate and environment for literacy and for recording and assessing development.

First meetings are always important and the first impressions that a young child has of school are crucial. The first meeting of child and teacher each day is also important as this is the transition point from home to school. The first suggestion for observation in this chapter is set, therefore, at the start of the school day.

Suggestion for observation
What happens to the young child first thing in the morning on arrival at school?

How is the start of the school day organized for the young child? Observe one child for about fifteen minutes at the very beginning of the school day.

Some points to consider
Does the child wait in the playground with a parent?

Do the child and parent come straight into the classroom where the teacher is waiting?

Is there any talk between the child and the teacher?

Comment

Parents and children often come straight into the classroom when they arrive at school. Parents may stay for a while or they may go leaving the child talking with the teacher or with friends or settled in an activity of their choice. If this is the picture then children will not only experience a stress-free introduction to each day at school but will have an opportunity to talk informally and individually to the teacher, probably about events at home.

Suggestion for observation
Sit back and listen quietly to a news or 'show and tell' session with the teacher and the whole class.

Listen carefully to the exchanges between teacher and child and between children at this time.

Points to consider
Commonly in infant classrooms one of the first class meetings of the day centres around children giving their 'news' or showing things they have brought in from home. There is no extended conversation in this situation — the whole event can be more like an unprepared 'performance' from the young child who either becomes inhibited by the realization of the situation or is prepared to give an extended monologue to an audience that is already becoming restless.

Comment

When observing the talk in the infant classroom it soon becomes obvious that:

1   it is difficult to organize a prolonged interaction between an individual child and the teacher;

2   whole class talk usually results in brief question and answer techniques.

Some teachers get around this situation by pairing children up and asking them to relate their news to a friend. The friend has to listen carefully and then be prepared to inform the rest of the group.

The pragmatic approach to the promotion of talk, and indeed to a large proportion of children's learning in the classroom, would seem to be to concentrate on small group activities and learning. Small groups are typically the organizational unit through which the teacher hopes to enable cognitive and social development.

Within a group of four or six, children may in fact be largely performing tasks and activities of their own. It is quite difficult for children of this age to sustain cooperation and discussion in a group. Often the best compromise is for children to work in pairs.

Encouragement and help to talk things through and interact with other children is constantly given. Talk is vital — both for social reasons and for children's learning.

Suggestion for observation
Watch and listen to a small group or a pair of young children engaged on a learning task together.

Try to think how their talking might be productive of their learning and also be a means for establishing themselves socially — it may be helpful to tape-record their talk.

Some points to consider
How much of the talk was concerned with the task in hand?

Was 'off-task' talk simply a waste of time, or was it serving other functions?

Comment

This kind of conscious planned situation is very different in its demands and unspoken messages from situations at home referred to in Chapter 3 where talk is largely unplanned and incidental. There is a very marked and special difference in the talk between teacher and child in school and the talk between adult and child outside the school context. Outside the child will often initiate the exchange on topics and concerns that are close to him/her and within the adult and child's shared experience. In the classroom the teacher usually initiates any exchange and often guides the talk towards an end point that she has in mind. It may be a solution to a problem, it may be to perceive a sequence of events, it may be to promote a particular awareness.

Up to this point, observations and comments have centred around children's talk in contexts that have been managed by the teacher. The teacher by explicit and implicit means seeks to develop children's oral language in and through learning activities and, conversely, to develop children's learning through talk, with her and with each other.

The child or children in the exchange soon realize that a particular outcome of their talk with the teacher is expected; they may then become inhibited and even choose not to venture a contribution at all in case it might be the 'wrong' one. This, in turn, leaves the teacher with impressions about the children's language and of their understanding.

Within the classroom there are contexts in which children can talk together where the direct or indirect influence of the teacher is much less apparent. The most obvious context for this is within the home corner or in a play area.

In this situation it is the children who initiate the talk. Often the area is partly hidden from the teacher's view which gives the added feeling of independence from the teacher's intentions.

Important situations for children's talk are often outside the four walls of the classroom. Break times are very significant in the school life of the young child. Although supervised by teachers or supervision assistants they are dominated by essentially child-initiated and centred talk and activity. The playground lacks the security of the home-corner and talk for regulating others, for self-maintenance and for affiliation is likely to be dominant.

As has been stated previously, there is much evidence of the impressive development of children's oral language in contexts that are easy and familiar where adult and child have common experiences and understanding. It is impossible to replicate this situation in the classroom and the teacher-child relationship may not be the best one for promoting children's spoken language.

A partial solution to this dilemma is for a good deal of paired work where children can genuinely help each other in exploratory and problem-solving learning situations. This talk for learning has to be nurtured and encouraged in young children and it becomes more effective as children become less egocentric. Teachers can present a model for interested listening and encouragement of exploratory talk which the children can emulate.

Another solution both to the problem of artificiality and to the problem of one teacher interacting with, say, thirty children is obvious. Other adults are needed in the classroom. Reference will be made later in the chapter to the role of other adults in reading and in writing and it is to cooperate with the teacher in these aspects of literacy that they are often invited in. As no aspect of literacy can be developed, nor should be developed, on its own, then these adult volunteers are necessarily engaging the children in conversations. They are seen by the children as having a different status from the teacher, there in the capacity of adult friends. In such a role the conversations are more likely to be balanced and rooted in topics and situations promoting genuine enquiry.

One very serious, cautionary note needs to be sounded here: part of the function of schooling as it stands is to assess children's language development, not only in terms of the individual development but also comparing one child with another or against some kind of norm. We do this by looking at the outward, visible signs. We should be very careful not to judge children's mental capability nor their potential for learning by their talk when they first come to school. The theme of assessment will be developed later in this chapter and again in the following chapter. It is most important, however, at this very early stage that teachers should not make premature decisions about a child's capabilities founded on the aspect of language that they can most readily assess — i.e. the child's talk. Enough has been written already in this book for the reader to be cautious — teacher-directed situations are not always the best contexts for many children to develop or exhibit their spoken language. You may have already gained some insight into this through your observations of interaction at home, in the home-corner and outside the confines of the classroom.

Focus on Reading

Talking to pre-school children and their parents about what they hope for from school, the answer they most often give is concerned with learning to read. This aspect of literacy is probably rated as the most important in the child's early years at school. Fluency in reading is the aim of both teacher and parent. Most children achieve this — but many adults read very little voluntarily beyond their years of schooling.

The main part of most adults' reading is short bursts of what is called 'functional' reading — this is to do with understanding written information for work, for self-maintenance and for citizenship. Much of this reading is in response to events and situations impinging on individuals and is not initiated by them. Many adults do not turn readily to print and text for information/interest, pleasure, satisfaction, escape. This end result may be reasonably satisfactory from a purely functional and social point of view for, say, 80–85 per cent of adults — but we must look very carefully at the 'means' by which this less than favourable situation arises. On the one hand there is a majority of adults who do not choose to read in any sustained way, and on the other hand a sizeable minority of adults whose literacy does not serve them well for their needs and interests in the work place, in their home and in their leisure.

The feelings that young children have about themselves as readers are formed by the way in which they come to reading and by the books that they first engage with. There will be pleasure and interest, or struggle, boredom and alienation — these factors must have an effect on their long-term attitudes towards reading for interest, satisfaction and pleasure. The long-term aim for teachers and parents at this early stage is that the experiences children have will be setting them up to be 'readers for life'. If these early experiences present reading as difficult, tedious or traumatic then it is unlikely that young adults at the end of schooling will read more than is necessary. It is also unlikely that children while growing and developing will have their lives enhanced and enriched by stories, poems and fascinating information.

Most of us recall very little of our early experiences in learning to read. Indeed, although there has been a lot of enlightenment in this area in recent years, we cannot be exactly sure of what the reading process entails.

Take a moment and try to remember any early recollections you have of learning to read or any behaviour that your parents might have recounted to you.

Points to consider

Unless you had difficulties in the early stages of learning to read you may probably recall very little of what happened. You are much more likely to remember things you read: books, stories, poems etc. The process of reading probably seems rather vague.

Some adults say that they learnt to read by 'sounding words out'. It is interesting that this feature of the learning process is the one open to recall and may well reflect that this task was problematical in some way. It is interesting to think that if we only used a phonic analysis strategy in learning to read we would take many years in the learning such are the irregularities of the English language sound system.

Example

Ann's mother used to recount to her an early experience in the process of learning to read. At 2 years old she would demand adults' attention by 'offering' to read to them. Her mother recalls that the milkman was a favourite target and had to pause from his busy round and be 'read' the same book, upside down each time. This is a good illustration of early reading behaviour showing that Ann knew the purposes of reading.

Very few children come to school with no experience of print and of reading. Until recently, though, when children started school at 4/5 they were all introduced to 'pre-reading' activities. These were seen as the foundation on which the reading of texts could be developed. Often the activities did not entail experiences with print or books but series of games, puzzles and exercises to develop concepts like left to right directionality and fine visual and auditory discrimination.

The idea that we need to break down the whole of reading as a language process into bite size chunks in order that children may digest them belongs to a behaviourist view of language.

This view is based on two premises:

1   That young children are taught language in a stimulus response situation with the adult/teacher providing the stimulus and the child always responding.

2   That language (in this case reading) can be broken down into identifiable skills or bundles of skills which can be taught in a hierarchical order.

More recently, there has emerged a completely different view of reading based on an analysis of what fluent readers do when reading.

This view of reading is based on two premises that run directly contrary to those of the previous skills-based model:

1   That young children are not taught language, they learn it in the context of a language community and in an environment saturated with it.

2   That language (in this case reading) is a holistic process — the whole being more than the sum of the parts — and cannot usefully be broken down into a series of hierarchical small steps.

Obviously the way in which the teacher perceives reading will determine the ways in which she will work with children in the classroom. The whole approach will be different, the texts and books offered to children will be different, the organization of time and materials will be different, the whole environment will be different.

Frank Smith (1978) states that in order for a child to learn to read there are two basic necessities. These are '. . . interesting material that makes sense to the learner and an understanding adult as a guide'.

Taking the 'interesting material that makes sense to the child' first, how could we interpret this in terms of books to read in the classroom and at home?

We know that children's minds, emotions and imaginations are engaged through story from a very early age.

A suggested task

Bearing in mind that what children read is important from the beginning and that they need to be engaged with the books they are offered . . .

Select five or six story books from those available in your classroom/library/bookshop that you think would be 'suitable' for the young beginner reader.

Try to list the attributes that you feel these books have.

Points to consider

Words — Should the story be made up of common sight words so that children build up a useful vocabulary or is the story content more important?

Pictures — Are these important in early books for children?

Storyline — Is a strong storyline important, or is this not possible in books for very young children?

Since the early mid-70s there has been a lot of rethinking about the reading process based mainly on three lines of exploration.

1   How children come to talk. This process has been charted and applied to the learning process in reading and writing.

2   What the fluent reader has to be able to do in order to read fluently.

3   How different texts can 'teach' children about reading and the way in which a strong story line and lively illustrations carry the reader along. (Meek, 1982; Smith, 1978)

From these three bases the importance of making meaning and being able to predict what comes next in reading emerges. Reading is no longer seen as a decoding print to sound exercise. The emphasis has shifted from teaching children to read to children learning to read (as they learn to talk). This change is important and far-reaching in all aspects of literacy and in learning as a whole. Language is not made up of a series of hierarchical skills but is holistic.

Children do not learn a language by starting with letters or sounds, building up to words which finally have meaning when combined together. Children's utterances when communicating have meaning from the start. They learn to talk from two basic premises:

1   They have something they need/want to communicate.
2   They have someone close to them that they need/want to communicate with — who will understand and extend their talk.

Children learn to talk in a social context — because they need to be part of a talking community. This social context needs to be present and to be developed in the classroom not only in talk but also in reading and writing. The whole environment and organization need to reflect a literate community which all can and want to join. The teacher him/herself is the prime mover in this microcosm of a literate society.

Pleasure and satisfaction in books and in reading must be there for the young child from the start.

This is vital for two reasons:

1   It is only in this way that children's whole learning processes will be engaged, their imagination, their emotion, their understanding of language, of real life and story situations, the motivation to read, the urge to share and enjoy with friends and with adults, their growing understanding of the pact between author and reader, their ability to predict and to retell, their ability to read and appreciate the illustrations.

   All these powerful factors operate together when a child engages with a book written by an author who develops the theme for a story. A good book, conceived and crafted by someone with a strong creative gift, will leave 'room' for the reader to create his own world inside his head. Such a book will be open to several levels of interpretation and response. Such a book will invite the reader to return, each time finding pleasure and satisfaction.

2   It is important that any learning process makes sense from the start. A child who is presented with instruction and texts that either confuse or bore him will either turn away from the whole process or proceed through extrinsic motivation, getting satisfaction only in finishing one level and moving onto another.

   Such texts are often difficult, not easy to read because they often do not allow for prediction, the most powerful learning strategy. They may not give children that vital engagement with the text. The text does not teach children to read and respond in different ways. The language used is neither book language nor spoken language written down.

   The lack of pace and tension and strong story line does not allow for re-reading. The hierarchy of texts invites competitiveness and feeling of failure, the structure of a scheme promotes the desire to 'finish' the books rather than discover the solution of a story or to dwell on fascinating pictures or to go back over and enjoy again favourite books.

Smith's second necessity for reading is 'an understanding adult as a guide'.

The first implication to consider from this is that the teacher is not the only 'understanding adult' available. Waterland (1985) writes about an apprenticeship in reading. This phase best sums up the practical expression of the reading process. Children learn about reading, about books and how to read alongside someone who will give them time and interest and who is themselves a reader.

The first adults to qualify in this respect must be the child's parents or caregivers. Many schools now are organizing for a partnership with parents in children's reading based within the home and/or within the classroom. The practice is now becoming well established. Parents are not taking over the teacher's role, they are just spending regular times sharing a book with their child after having been given advice and guidance from the teacher (Bloom, 1987).

Smith (1978) states 'Children learn to read by reading'; this is a truism and yet a paradox. Clearly an essential element in the learning of any process is practice in doing it. Yet children come to the reading process at first unable to do it. This suggests that the first step is that children be read to and with. Children are natural learners. They will gradually join in with the reading and, when they are able, take over the reading for themselves. If they can see the point in reading, if the experiences and the books are satisfying and promising they will want to become independent in their reading so that they can control the situation.

In many infant classrooms other people besides the teacher help children with learning to read. Parents of children in the class are obvious candidates here. There may be arrangements for other members of the local community to come regularly and share books with children. Sometimes older children within the school partner young children in an infant class and they read and talk about books regularly together. Friends within the classroom get together and share a book, the more experienced reader taking the lead, gaining much confidence and showing in many ways the power of being able to read.

Of course, young children like to have their own time set aside to read with the teacher. These are occasions when they will talk about a book, perhaps read together or in turns, or the teacher will start by reading to the child. The child will be encouraged to predict likely events and to recall past events, to discuss the pictures. The book chosen may well be a familiar one, in which case the child might take over the reading. Sometimes the child will be encouraged to predict or guess words he doesn't know. This is a valuable opportunity for the teacher to think about the strategies the child is using.

The classroom is the centre of a literate community — all the children are members — either full or intending members. There is a social context for reading. Another manifestation of the social context of reading is when the teacher reads a book to the class.

Sometimes she will read and the children will join in from an oversize book (Holdaway, 1979) so that she can demonstrate many factors about books and reading while the whole group is engaged with the story. Afterwards there are small copies for children to read to themselves. They are already familiar with the book and will soon read it.

Sometimes the teacher will read from the collection of books that the children will want to be reading independently. Again, apart from enjoying the shared experience of the story they will be familiarizing themselves with the story and with the words in which the story is conveyed — a kind of group apprenticeship in reading.

These 'familiar' books may well be stored together for children to select from and read independently when they spend time in the book corner. Children need the satisfaction and security that comes from this, they will build up gradually the repertoire of books they can read for themselves. These books and others might be taped so that children can listen and read.

Sometimes the teacher will select a book that none of the children would at that moment be able to read independently. She is giving the children experiences of stories that they could not gain for themselves. Often from these sessions other activities develop: writing class, group or individual stories, telling the story with pictures, improvizing a play.

Sometimes the teacher will select a book without words and the children will 'read' the illustrations and talk their way through the story.

Reading to the class is so important, particularly at this stage of a child's reading development. Children are learning, too, the language with which to talk about books but this learning is incidental, just a part of the shared reading experience which is relaxed and enjoyable.

Reading and writing go together. One of the most important sources of children's reading is their own writing or stories which they have dictated to an adult helper or to the teacher, either individually or as a class or group. These books will also form part of the book corner collection of books.

Books are not the only sources of children's reading and of their becoming readers. The classroom can provide an environment for print in a similar way to the shops and streets outside. There are notices, reminders, lists, captions, labels, instructions, warnings, all giving opportunities for informational reading to complement the story and poem reading.

A Focus on Writing

As previously mentioned it is unlikely that children will come to school with no experience of writing. They will have seen parents and other writers in their family and community writing in various contexts for different purposes. Parents and others write and receive letters — leave notes for each other, make lists, fill in forms, send away for things, copy down information.

Becoming a fluent independent writer — like becoming reading — a fluent independent reader — is a gradual process which takes a considerable time. As with reading, the early experiences are crucial for the child's development of concepts, skills and attitudes.

What do young children need . . .?
An awareness of the purpose of print is obviously necessary.
Young children need to realize that the marks on the page carry a message — that there is an intention behind them.

Children's spoken language needs to be well developed as it is this ability that they bring to the beginnings of writing.

Experiences of written texts. The more young children are read to the more they will understand the forms of written language. Writing is very different from speech and through reading and being read to and through writing itself children gradually establish the differences.

Opportunities to write, to experiment and play with words or letters, confidence to take risks as they learn.

Guidance, help, encouragement and support from the teacher in different ways, from individual help with a piece of writing they want to do to demonstration and talk with a group or with the whole class.

Lastly young children have the manipulative aspect of writing to contend with. The cognitive demands of reading and writing are similar but writing carries with it the added physical demand of manipulating the writing instrument while organizing and memorizing what is to be written. At the earliest stages children will need instruction and guidance on letter formation as they begin to experiment with writing.

To alleviate these demands and enable them to produce texts that are larger than they could manage independently, children need an adult or experienced writer to write for them sometimes.

Children's early writing in school will be very close to their spoken language in its structure and in the invented spelling of the words. It is a long and sometimes arduous road between first attempts at writing and the 'ultimate' capability to write independently in different ways for different purposes.

Suggestion for reflection
Think back over the last week. What have you written during this period? Take a few minutes and list as many things as you can remember.

Points to consider
Some of the writing you engaged in will have been in some form of communication with other people across time and distance with notes, forms and requests. Some of the writing will have been for yourself, reminders and lists, notes from reading or from talks, aide-memoires from meetings or perhaps diary entries. (It is interesting to think that most adults do not engage in any imaginative writing.)

The writing that we do has a purpose and a reader and we hold these two factors in our mind as we write. They affect the style, the format and the content of our writing. For instance, there will be a vast difference between a letter to a close friend which is written almost like a one-way conversation and a letter of application for a job.

Sometimes the writing is intended for ourselves and is part of the learning process. We write and we trigger off recollections from our memory, we read the writing and are able to reformulate our thinking as a consequence. Thus writing can be a powerful tool in our learning.

Suggestion for observation
Gather together a child's writing over a week. (This should include writing done at home if possible.)

Points to consider

Look at the variety of the writing. Were there different formats, different styles and was the writing sometimes intended for readers other than the teacher?

Comment

A week is a short time so that your sample may not be representative. It is important, though, for young children to have opportunities to write in different ways so that their writing from the beginning reflects the purposes and the power of writing.

Purposes for Writing

There are many different purposes for writing in the infant classroom — the teacher is constantly offering situations and taking up ideas for writing from the children themselves. Probably the two most common contexts for writing in the early years are news and story. Children talk about then draw and write about events that surround them and their families. They also readily compose stories based on what they have read/had read to them — and from TV programmes.

Sometimes writing may be done by the teacher, by groups or individually. Someone in the classroom will be away ill — here is an opportunity to write letters or make get well cards — festivals and special occasions in school are signalled and recalled in writing. Thank you letters after class visits, writing away for information, writing to authors, this kind of writing to 'unknown audiences' is part of a writing repertoire which the child develops with help and encouragement from the class teacher. Inside the classroom itself children share their stories and poems with each other, they write about science experiments for each other's information, they write instructions on how to look after the gerbil; notices about forthcoming events, dinner menus or special arrangements, messages to each other and to the teacher.

The situations and purposes for writing may be rich and varied. Children are part of a writing community, they are constantly being reminded of the purposes and potential of written text. How, though, do young children come to write? What kind of approaches are there available for the teacher to consider? As with learning to read there has been a recent growing understanding of the writing process. The traditional approach was based on copying and practice. The teacher would write for the child and the child would firstly write over, then trace over, then copy underneath, then copy from one page to another and then copy from the blackboard and finally start to embark on their own efforts at writing.

There has been a lot of work and observation done with emergent young writers and it seems clear that given a writing environment, being surrounded by print and having their attention drawn to it, receiving support and encouragement from the teacher and being with others who write — children come through the writing process in a series of definite stages that could be equated with stages in early talk and reading. In the early stages of writing, following such an approach, children will experiment with spelling.

Suggestion for observation
Sit with a young, inexperienced writer while he writes freely. Try to note down what you think your writer knows about writing.

Points to consider
You may be able to recognize individual words or letters. The writing may be arranged from left to right in lines across the page. The writer will be able to 'read' his writing to you, it is interesting to ask the writer to identify a specific part of the writing. The writer will appreciate that the writing carries meaning and relates to spoken language.

Comment on Jenny's writing
(The teacher wrote down what Jenny said she had written in order to be able to study it more closely afterwards.)

Jenny understands that writing goes from left to right and is arranged in lines filling the width of the page.

She seems to have the beginnings of 'I went' above the first line of writing and it looks as though she changed her mind about the opening words. She pointed to 'a' below the second line for 'and'.

She knows and can write quite a lot of letters but does not yet group them into words. She has the idea, though, that information can be written down and can be 'read' sometime later.

She enjoyed her writing!

Probably the first word that children will write consistently is their name, from the sound/letter correspondence they will extract sounds for this and other words that they become familiar with to construct new words. It seems likely that children's acuity for some

Writing Example

Jenny, nearly 5 years old, in her second term at school. (Free choice of subject.)

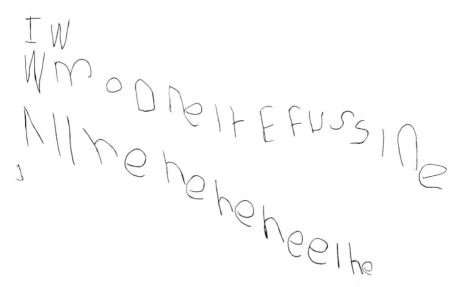

One day I went to my little Nan's and it was sunny.

sounds within spoken words develops earlier than for others. Hard consonants are easier to pick up in speech and these may be the letters within words on the page that children attend to first — initial sounds stand out more than middle or final sounds so that at an early stage children may just write consonants to signify a whole word.

Long vowels are also noticed more easily than short ones and so the process goes on — writing together as a class with the teacher transcribing and children composing, attending to individual words within their own stories and on notices, labels, captions inside and outside the classroom. Reading, writing go hand in hand surrounded by the talk of exploration, explanation, encouragement and elaboration.

Through many and varied opportunities, through guidance and support and most importantly through confidence in themselves and engagement in the writing task — young children gradually become aware through their reading and writing of two important factors:

1   the consistency of spelling;
2   the reader.

When children first write they are probably unaware of these two elements in the writing process, they have too much to concentrate on in:

1   the manipulative aspect; and
2   bringing and holding their thoughts together long enough to express them on paper. They are naturally egocentric in their writing, finding enough satisfaction in making marks on the page.

Having an audience for their writing gives reason for consistency in spelling, but this dawning understanding can bring about tension. The children may be inhibited when they realize that their efforts at spelling do not coincide with standard spelling. This can be an enormous growth point as this awareness is refined and children gradually appreciate the fine differences and their spelling approximates more and more closely to standard spelling.

If on the other hand correctness is emphasized too soon the emerging writers may falter at this stage — the awareness of the task before them becoming too heavy and writing becoming an activity accompanied by apprehension and anxiety.

An Environment for Writing

Consider the classroom and how it can offer different opportunities and purposes for children to write, together with examples of writing.

Is there a domestic corner in the room? Does it include examples of writing — newspapers, directories, recipes, etc.? Is there a telephone pad for messages — a pad for shopping lists with writing tools? Shops, cafes, travel agencies, post offices all these 'play' situations give rise to purposeful situations for writing.

Is there a place — a corner or a 'book' — where children can choose to sit and write freely? Are there writing tools, different papers, examples of writing — sources of useful words there?

Are there notices, instructions, captions and labels that children can read and respond to?

Is there a comfortable book corner with lively books and opportunity to read privately, with a friend, or with an experienced reader? Are children's own books written or dictated by them included in the collection?

The classroom can provide a 'print rich' environment for children, offering opportunity to write and experiment with writing in many different ways. Collections of useful words and later clear dictionaries can help children to be independent of the teacher. The way in which time and space are managed by the teacher is important, too.

The Development of Children's Writing in the Infant Classroom — Content Range and Secretarial Skills

The content, punctuation, grammar of written language, as well as spelling and clear handwriting develop as reading and awareness of the audience develops. The sentence is a written convention only — we don't speak in sentences. Young writers gradually come to the understanding that writing must carry the whole meaning of the message. When talking in conversation the speaker relies on the listener understanding the message without it being 'spelt out'. The speaker uses gesture and facial expression and studies the response of the listener, together they make the meaning clear. If the talker and listener have a shared life and common experiences, as do parents and children, then much of the content of the conversation is implied. This cannot be the case with writing, but children can only gradually develop an awareness and response to this.

Story writing and 'news' writing may form a large proportion of early writing. These forms of writing have their own understood structure and form. Accounts of events near to the child are usually dealt with chronologically in early writing. Stories have a well-recognized pattern of introduction, development, climax and resolution, this form being so strong in children's early reading experiences.

Other forms of writing especially informational writing are mastered later in the young child's writing experience. They have much more subtle internal structures and the young writer has to impose his/her own control over the form of such writing.

Publishing Writing

It is important that children's writing is valued and as they develop as writers that they have readers, starting from the situation where the class create a story for the teacher to transcribe — or individual children go through the same process with an adult and moving on to when children take on more responsibility for their own writing.

Some pieces of writing may be gathered together under a theme and be displayed or collected within a book. Often there will be accompanying illustrations — sometimes the child will write a story that is typed up and illustrated — the resulting book is displayed in the book corner and may be chosen and read alongside commercially published books.

Children often collaborate in writing with a pair or small group sharing the task — there is obviously much reading and talking accompanying the intention to produce a story for others to read.

The teacher is an enabler in this situation, joining the discussion — encouraging in the proof-reading, judging when to offer help and when to stand back, whether the work should be perfect or acceptable and readable.

The role of the teacher is crucial for young children developing as writers. The core of the teacher's work is with individual writers, encouraging, helping, guiding while they write. Useful records need to be kept so that the teacher can reflect on the next step for each writer.

Other adults and/or experienced writers have their part to play under the guidance of the classteacher, they can read and write with the young writer, can write for them, can type up a final copy of writing to be read by others, can talk about the child's intentions for the writing.

Parents/caregivers at home can also take on these functions with guidance and encouragement from the teacher and can be readers for some of the writing that their child does in school.

The teacher also has a role of demonstrator, writing on behalf of the class or of a group on large paper so that children can see words being formed. They can understand the directionality, see the spacing between the words and recognize some letters and sounds within words. The teacher also provides guidance and instruction for letter formation, both in demonstration and in providing and organizing resources to help children in this.

The teacher is the orchestrator of the print rich classroom environment, for support resources for writing, for storage and retrieval of writing materials, for organizing the publication of children's writing, for making sure that children have opportunities to write in different ways for different purposes for different readers.

The teacher also needs to be a role model for the young writers in her class. They need to see her writing — notes to colleagues, to them, to parents, short pieces or poems to share with them when they are engaged on this kind of writing, reminders on the blackboard or on the class bulletin board.

Conclusion

This chapter has been concerned with children's developing powers of literacy in the infant school. Most children come to school with well developed spoken language and often with experience of reading and writing. The task of the teacher is to build on the language they bring to school with them. Talking, listening, reading and writing are constantly interwoven and develop hand in hand. There are three important agents in this development.

1   The child, who is an active learner and will experiment, query and hypothesize.
2   The teacher (and other interested adults), who will guide, teach, give examples, support and encourage.
3   The environment for literacy of the classroom and school, which provides materials, models, purposes, time, space and opportunities.

For the infant years, 'literacy in action' is a very apt slogan!

Chapter 5

Starting in the Junior School — The First Two Years

In their seventh year most children move on to the second stage in their schooling — they go from infants to juniors. The move may not be very far — just along the corridor, perhaps, or it may be to a separate junior school. This is an important point in their school lives.

This chapter is concerned with children's first two years in the junior school.

It might be helpful at this stage to pose two questions:

(i) What are teachers' expectations of children coming into the junior school?
(ii) What do children bring with them from their infant school experience?

The answers to these two questions may be identical or there may be a discrepancy between them.

What Are the Teachers' Expectations?

Teachers would probably hope that most, if not all children will have progressed past the initial stages of reading and writing and will be becoming independent in these areas. Students deciding whether to opt for infant or junior work often give this as being the prime factor in their choice. They are either more interested in working with children at the beginnings of literacy and being part of the rapid development which takes place at this stage or more interested in being able to build on this foundation and to help children widen and deepen their learning.

The National Curriculum document *English for Ages 5 to 11* has listed attainment targets that most children at age 7 should have reached (DES, 1988).

Not all the points refer to attainment; attitudes such as interest, confidence are mentioned. Teachers are very concerned that children should develop positive attitudes to literacy. If they do, then the likelihood that they will enjoy and be engaged in literacy all their lives is much higher.

What Literacy Experiences Are These Attainments Resting On?

In Reading

. . . a rich experience of story and rhyme. Much of this rich experience will be built up through listening to the teacher, other adults, other children and caregivers at home. Much of it will be shared, some of it may be one-to-one, especially at home.

. . . reading books of their own choosing. By 7 most children will be developing preferences in fiction, though these will shift as they are introduced to new authors and different genres. These preferences will be based on characters, genre, style and illustrations, writer and initially on the interest and attractiveness of the cover.

Children will be used to returning to old favourites for enjoyment and security. The attractive book corners that feature in so many infant classrooms will have had an influence on children's attitude to reading.

. . . listening to tapes. Children can enhance their enjoyment and understanding of books by listening to tapes alongside the reading or without the book. Mostly children will have been able to widen their reading experience by listening to tapes and following a story that they would not be able to read independently. They will quickly learn to operate the tape recorder and by this means be able to control their listening and reading without adult help.

. . . reading 'environmental' writing. Children will have experienced a good deal of informational reading through charts, captions, posters, shop/domestic/cafe corner.

Children's reading experiences will not be confined to the classroom and to school, much of their learning will have been going on at home and in their environment generally.

In Writing

. . . a good deal of personal and expressive writing will have been attempted. Children will usually have tried to write stories too.

. . . other kinds of writing will have been introduced for reporting, accounting, instructing, listening and sending messages. The personal and expressive voice will still be evident in the writing, but children of 7 are becoming aware that different kinds of writing are suited to different kinds of purposes.

. . . illustrating their writing. Traditionally very young writers have drawn first and written about the drawing afterwards with help from the teacher. As children are being encouraged more and more to experiment with writing for themselves they are less dependent and may well use drawings to illustrate the writing as well as to initiate it.

Children coming to the junior stage at 7 will have been used to attempting individual writing, of writing with a friend, and with adults. They will be used to 'composing' in collaboration with the rest of the class for the teacher to transcribe, demonstrating any aspects of writing while doing so.

Keeping Records

What teachers hope to do in the early junior stages is to build on the foundations of literacy laid down through good infant practice. Junior teachers are endeavouring to widen and deepen children's experiences and understandings in literacy. This process is enabled by factors in the teaching and learning opportunities offered to the child and also by factors in children's development, and by the child's own increasing experience of literacy.

Junior teachers' expectations and children's attainments and attitudes will be synonymous (or nearly so) if regular and sensitive records are kept and handed on at the time of transfer. Children are very different at 7 in their achievements, understandings, attitudes and preferences. Good communication is essential if the move is to be smooth and junior teachers able to build on children's previous learning.

Suggested observation task
Look at the ways in which records are kept and handed on and the ways in which teachers in infant and junior classes communicate. Are

the records sufficiently detailed to be of real use to receiving teachers? Are examples of children's writing included with evaluative comments? Is there any kind of indication of children's reading experiences, preferences, difficulties?

Comment

Of course not all valuable information can be conveyed in writing — teachers need to talk to each other both informally and in a planned and prepared way as the time comes near for transfer. It is very useful too, if the receiving teacher in the junior school can go into the top infant class and work with the children. This gives a realistic insight into the way children are operating.

Having set the scene and moved the children from the infant to the early junior stages the rest of the chapter will be addressed to a focus on reading, a focus on writing and a brief consideration of the role of oral language in the final part. Of course, in practice, reading and writing, talking and listening are seldom completely separated. It can be useful, however, to concentrate on the two different aspects, reading and writing, go in more depth and then to draw it all together to demonstrate the breadth and the wholeness of the language experience.

A Focus on Reading

The early junior stage is a time for getting children 'hooked on books'. This is a time when their attitudes to reading are set, perhaps for life.

Why Do We Read? What Can Books Do For Us?

Teachers set such a store by encouraging children to be 'readers for life'. What do we get from books that is so precious and important? We can get insights into other people's lives and other worlds; we can travel back and onward in time; we can understand 'truths' that cannot be given in any other form; we can appreciate the writer's craft and the best use of writing language. We can derive satisfaction, pleasure, pain, relief, laughter, curiosity, resolution, escape, question and information — so much out of so versatile a resource. We can read books on trains and buses, in bed, in the bath, in the garden, on the beach. Not everyone derives so much from reading, but every child has the right to.

The Books that Children Read

What do children read?

It is important to get a clear picture of children's preferences in their reading so that you can suggest titles that children might be interested in. The range of their reading also needs to be considered. Could they benefit from being introduced to different genres?

Suggested observation task
The questionnaire below is an example of one way in which you could try to find out more about a child's reading preferences and habits. You might go through this with a child or children. Perhaps they could take it home to complete. A 7-year-old and his teacher discussed the questionnaire and together they produced the following:

Name: Peter   *Class:* 1   *Date:* 14/12/88

What Do You Read?

1 What book are you reading now?
   a)   at home: *Nothing*
   b)   at school: *Funtime*
2 What is the best book you have read recently?
        Funtime. I like it.
3 What is the best book you have ever read, or heard read?
        The BMX Race. Ross's mummy read it in the library.
4 What kind of reading do you prefer?
   Finding out. Poems. Stories. Comics. Magazines. Newspapers.
5 Do you go to the library to borrow books?
   No. Sometimes. Often. Every week.
6 How many books of your own do you have at home?
   A few. About 20. More than 20.
   About 10 and some comics.
7 Do you prefer to read at home or at school. *At school.*
   Can you give a reason? *Because you learn more things at school.*
8 Do you read with anyone at home?
   Who do you read with?   *My daddy and my mum and my brother.*
9 What do you read at home apart from books?

a) Comics ... Which ones? *Mummy reads Ghostbusters.*
A Lion comic.

b) Magazines ... Which ones?

c) Newspapers ... Which ones?

Which parts do you read? *Mummy reads them to me and my brothers. I keep looking at the papers and she keeps turning over too quick.*

d) Radio and TV Times?

Comment

It would seem that children of this age often choose their most recently read or heard book as their favourite! It would be a good idea, perhaps, to get Peter and other children to be regular borrowers from the public library as well as making times when they take home and read books from school. He does not state a preference for reading stories or poetry and, while children's preferences must be respected and built upon, the teacher should also be trying to encourage them to read fiction by picking out and recommending books to them.

Many teachers like to complete this kind of activity with children near the beginning of the school year in order to establish quickly an overall view of children's reading. This can help in pointing the way to introducing new titles or authors, and to see how regularly children read at home.

There may be a discrepancy between children's reading at home and at school that comes to light while responding to a questionnaire like this. An example arose recently when a teacher did this questionnaire with a 9-year-old boy, who was reading for the main part Ginn 360 Level 4 in school. He had been reading *Wind in the Willows* at home! Further questioning established that he was reading the greater part of the book independently getting help from his parents when he needed it. He had decided to read the book after a recent school visit to the theatre showing the play of the book. The way in which he talked about the book made it obvious that he had derived meaning and a lot of enjoyment from the book.

Children who are becoming independent in their reading will show a wide variation in their preferences. They are becoming discriminating readers, able and willing to talk about the books they enjoy. They are coming to the stage where they want to follow up on a particular writer or a kind of book that they are enjoying over a period of time. Some children at this stage start showing a preference for non-fiction gaining much satisfaction and pleasure from this source.

Knowing about Children's Books

As a teacher trying to get children 'hooked' on books there would seem to be two overriding concerns:

(i) to know as many books as possible;
(ii) to know as much as possible about the children in the class as readers.

By bringing these two areas of knowledge together the teacher is able to match the books to the child.

Children, who at this time are not able to read many books independently being at an earlier stage in their reading development need this skill of matching perhaps more than the other children. They need the familiarity and security of texts that they can enjoy independently and chances to experience a wider range of books without support. This support in a wider range of reading can come from a more experienced reader — the teacher reading to the class, or another adult — or from a book tape. It is very important that this group of children is kept in touch with the satisfactions and pleasures of reading so that they don't lose sight of the reasons for their efforts to master it.

Resources and Environment for Reading

Every school has a slightly different system for storing and accessing the books they make available for children.

Suggested observation task
Where can children choose books from in a school? Note down the various access points and what kinds of books there are available at each one.

Example
A particular junior school stored their non-fiction books in a roomy, comfortable and well lit library room. Fiction books were kept in classroom book corners.

Comment

Most junior schools have a collection of books in each classroom and a centralized collection in a library room or area. Both sources may contain fiction and non-fiction as well as other non-book-based material.

The book collection in the classroom is the most readily accessible source of reading. It is important, too, that children have ready access to the centralized collection of books. Sometimes a library serves other purposes as well, for TV, small group work with a support teacher, computer work.

Ideally children should be able to use the library as and when the need arises. This free access is more readily available if there is an adult in the library able to supervise and help. Often schools have a group of parent volunteers who will do this. Some school libraries are available to children during lunch time. Again, this needs supervision, but it can give some children a valuable opportunity to relax and enjoy a good read or to follow up their particular interests, etc.

It is good if the library or book area can be a welcoming and comfortable place with work areas and floor cushions. Focus displays can be arranged featuring, perhaps, books written by children, new additions, certain writers.

Many schools make books available to children in other ways, perhaps through a school bookshop which may be run by parents, teachers and children in collaboration. Some schools receive regular mailings from book clubs, and children order books from a termly catalogue. Other schools have links with their local public library and encourage their children to be regular borrowers.

An attractive book corner is as important in a junior classroom as in an infant one. If space allows the area could be partially secluded and equipped with floor cushions and/or armchairs and carpeting. This area can be for children to choose books, spend time reading, listening to a tape, sharing books with a friend.

Children themselves, with guidance from the teacher, can be responsible for maintaining the book corner. Although the collection of books will not be extensive the arrangement needs to be inviting. Children can be responsible for a small focus display as in the centralized collection.

There are many attractive and humorous posters available promoting the reading habit, these can be displayed in the book corner, perhaps alongside children's own promotional material.

Tapes to accompany books can be located in the book corner. These are invaluable and very popular. Children, teachers and parents could be involved in taping some stories and poems. If headphones are available children can listen and read without being disturbed and without disturbing the rest of the class in quiet reading times.

Armchairs and cushions are much in demand at class reading time. Some teachers establish a rota for this adding to the 'pleasure factor' in reading. Contingency plans have to be laid for occasions when someone is absent and the vacancy disputed!

A collection of book reviews and recommendations is useful when children are not sure about their next choice and the teacher is not available. The reviews can be published ones or compiled by other children. Periodically children can be asked to write a brief review of a book they have particularly enjoyed for this purpose. They should not be expected to do this automatically after completing a book, as this can become a tedious chore. Quick comment cards are also helpful and easy to fill in — they might look like this.

Initials	"CITY SUMMER"
	Comments
SL	I liked the city summer very it was a good story and I am glad they brought me
KB	I like the last story about match of the day it was very good.
TS	I liked match of the day when she got took off the pitch.

JM
I like the last story match of the day it was good.

IG
I liked the last story and it was called match of the day.

SA
I liked the first story city summer it was very good

JC
I liked the mach of the day story

. . . These together with longer reviews can be placed strategically in the book area so that they are easily referred to when children select their books.

What Should Children Read at this Age?

In the National Curriculum Report, *English for Ages 5 to 11*, 200 writers are recommended for primary school children (DES, 1988). This is, of course, a suggested list not a prescriptive one. Often finances limit the number of books the school can buy. Within schools part of the classroom collections are often exchanged. LEAs have central collections that can be borrowed, usually for a term and provision is made for bulk ordering. Paperbacks are obviously a more economical buy, but all classroom collections should contain some hardback books. They have a very different 'feel' and a much more attractive format.

Different Levels of Reading

When we (or children) choose something to read we do not always look for material that challenges our understanding nor do we select material in an ever increasing level of difficulty. Sometimes we select material that is 'easy' for odd moment reading or for sheer escapism. Comics sometimes fulfil the same need for children, although 'reading' the strips in comics is not always easy. The appeal of comics is in the established characters and the predictability of their actions and reactions together with the colourful format. The worrying feature of some comics is the stereotyping of race and gender and in some comics the seeming glorification of war and violence.

Schools hold varying views on the acceptability of comics within a classroom collection, nevertheless they do play an important part in many children's voluntary reading.

Junior age children have favourite books that they first read or had read to them when they were younger. These kinds of books need to be included in the collection. Sometimes the re-reading brings back with it associated memories of the time when it was first encountered. These books will also be a valuable source of reading for children who are still at an earlier stage. They do need to be incorporated within the overall arrangement of books and not kept on a separate shelf otherwise children might feel diffident about choosing them.

There is a growing number of picture books for older children that are well worth including in any collection of books. The pictures, themes and texts are at a level that older children find satisfying. Here children 'read' the pictures more than the texts. Anthony Browne's books are a good example of this genre.

There are so many good writers for children that it may be more difficult to know what to exclude rather than include in a classroom collection. Note should be taken of children's current preferences and of current influences such as children's and school's TV.

Colour Coding

Sometimes schools arrange books into broad bands of difficulty. Teachers may decide the levels for themselves or may use published guides to do this. Children are either directed or advised to choose a book at the appropriate level(s) for them. These levels are indicated by giving the book a colour sticker. Often when they have read a certain number of books at one level they may progress to the next one. This system offers a framework for teachers and children.

Collecting books within broad bands of difficulty in this way is often a move away from following a structured reading scheme. It does give children an indication of which books they should be able to read independently, but also limits their choice. Often children will gain a lot of pleasure and satisfaction from a book that might be considered too difficult because they are really interested in the theme, the character or the author. Conversely, children may well want to read books allocated to a 'lower' colour, but feel reluctant to be seen selecting from this.

Reading Schemes

Some junior schools retain a reading scheme or schemes for some or all of their children. This may well be a continuation of a scheme started in the infant school. Although such an arrangement does offer structure to teachers and children the arguments against it remain much the same as those discussed in relation to the infant school. It seems a high price to pay for a notion of planned progression that does not seem to line up with theories of language development.

Time for Reading

It's obviously of limited value to provide an attractive book corner and a lively collection of books if no time is given to read them. It is true that many children do have opportunity to read at home, but teachers cannot rely on this happening. The actual process of reading is so valuable that it needs a recognized and regular place within the classroom activities.

Many schools arrange for children to have a set time for reading every day as well as other opportunities when children might choose to read. Directly after lunch break for 20–30 minutes is a favoured arrangement as children can prepare for this immediately before lunch. This is a time when children can settle and enjoy something they have chosen to read. Often the teacher reads alongside the children. This may seem indulgent but seeing the teacher engrossed in a 'good read' provides the children with a strong message about books and reading. The teacher might choose and read books from the classroom collection and be able to recommend them.

The material that children choose at this time will represent a level of reading that they are comfortable with, an independent level where little, or no, help is needed.

It is important that reading in this way is seen as an integral part of children's life at school and not as an odd-moment activity. If children only read during register time and when they have completed other tasks they would:

(a) see reading as being of marginal importance; or

(b) in the case of some children who rarely complete tasks, have little opportunity for chosen reading.

Suggested observation
A quiet reading time is often a good time to observe children's reading behaviour.

Look again at the children with whom you conducted a reading interview. Watch carefully and note how they prepare for and settle down to the reading. Note whether you think they were able to become engrossed in the reading.

Example
Eight-year-old Robert at the beginning of the year never seemed to be ready for reading time. On coming in after lunch he would rush to the book corner and scoop up a shelf full of supplementary readers and sit down just as everyone was settling quietly. He would often then go through the stack of books in rapid succession — flicking through and putting each one aside with a flourish. This might take 5 minutes of the 20 minutes alloted time and after that he would be anxious to go back to the corner for more books.

Comment

In his first school Robert had read books through two reading schemes almost exclusively. He was not able to get into these books and was starting to give up on becoming an independent reader. He had rarely been able to select what he wanted to read and was at first, completely thrown by the notion of choice. He was enthralled by a story when the teacher read to the class. The teacher spent some time helping and encouraging him to select books that he wanted to read. Some of his favourite books were on tape and by listening and reading he was gradually able to sustain the reading of a whole book. He gradually came to see what reading could offer him and though his choice of independent reading was limited he did begin to behave like a reader.

Reading to the Class

There is a strong tradition and practice of reading to the class in the infant school. Sometimes, however, junior school teachers are not so convinced of the value of this as they see most children becoming independent in their reading.

When some junior age children responded to a questionnaire recently the majority of them stated that they did appreciate being read to by their teacher. Many of them included remarks like 'she makes it more interesting' or 'she's got a good voice for reading' (for a fuller account see Bloom, Martin and Waters, 1988).

The books that teachers choose to read to the class will tend to be longer than those chosen in the earlier years. Most books will be read as a serial which means that the readings must be frequent in order to maintain the impact of the story. Reading to the class shouldn't always be scheduled at the end of the day even though this is a favoured time and has the effect of bringing the class together and winding up the day on a positive note. Often, though, other activities run over time and the story session gets squeezed out. Also children can respond in a more lively way and discuss more keenly earlier in the school day.

There are so many good books nowadays that it is very difficult to select those few that will be shared with the whole class. It is a good idea to think ahead over the course of a year and plan to present different genres to the children to give them a balanced diet. The first criterion for deciding must be that the teacher likes the story and can get it across well. The book must be 'worth' the time given to it. Going back to levels of reading the highest level that children experience might well be through the teacher reading to them. This enables children to reach that little bit further than they would attempt independently.

There are many considerations that might come into the choice. A play on children's TV might be followed up by reading the book, which can open up discussion about the differences between the two media.

Often after the teacher has read a book to the class she will offer it for children to read on their own. Many children like to do this, perhaps skimming through the story and reading closely the parts they particularly remember. There is often a queue of customers for books like this. A lending list can be put up on the class notice board with children ticking their names off after completing the book and passing it on to the next borrower. Something that has to be waited for can seem more precious!

Poetry must have its place at these sessions. Poems might be presented thematically or from the collection of a single writer. Poetry sessions do not need to be very long and it is often a good idea to have shorter odd moments in addition where one single well-liked poem can be presented. Of course, with poetry there is opportunity for audience participation in a variety of ways.

Sometimes story telling can take the place of reading or a story might be part-read with embellishments suited to a particular audience. As with young children visual aids can enhance the telling and children can be asked to participate. Children really value this shared experience and it is well worth while building up even a limited repertoire. Taking on different voices can add to the children's enjoyment. Care must be taken so that the visual effects do not take over from the story. One teacher recently gave a riveting opening to *The Iron Man* by Ted Hughes by spraying a rubber glove silver and using a marble for one of the lost eyes. The children were transfixed, waiting for the next dramatic visual effect and become very disappointed in the whole story when nothing else materialized!

Individual Reading with the Teacher

Younger junior children will be spending most of their reading time in reading silently. Nevertheless they need and still appreciate the individual attention of the teacher to talk with about books they have enjoyed, what they are reading now and to perhaps get ideas for what they might read next. This kind of individual meeting might take place once a fortnight. To help the teacher to keep track of the child's reading and to form a basis for talking together the child might keep up a simple book-log like the one below.

Children who are at an earlier stage in their reading development will still need to be sharing books with the teacher or other experienced readers and will need to do this much more frequently.

Informational Reading

In the document *English for Ages 5 to 11* this kind of reading is defined as 'the development of reading and information retrieval strategies for the purposes of study' (DES, 1988).

Although this section will be devoted to helping children to acquire and develop these strategies, there are times when children

Date	Title	Author	Finished/ Not finished	Liked it No/a bit/ a lot	Teacher's comment

A simple book-log.

want to browse through an information book without a specific purpose or time when they just want to learn from the illustrations and captions.

The following chapter devoted to literacy in the older junior stage will deal with informational reading in more depth. Younger junior children will be making a start on this kind of reading and they will vary considerably in how successfully they develop efficient and effective strategies.

Most of the children's individual reading in the infant school is from stories. The way in which readers approach information books is very different from story reading. Children rarely skip parts of a story or read the ending first, they are carried along by the events in the story which are often ordered chronologically. This order and structure applies to their writing, too. Information is organized in a very different way: it does not have an opening, character development, plot development, climax and resolution as story does. Often information books could be reorganized without detracting from their impact or meaning.

Suggested observation task
Try to observe a child you have observed previously as he/she reads an information book.

Try to start the observation when the child opens the book for the first time, then you will be able to see the whole process the child goes through.

Example

A Child Reading an Information Book

Title: *Garden Birds*

1. Book fell open near the middle — child looks carefully at bright colour photograph of bullfinch on apple blossom (does not read caption).
2. Goes back to title page — reads title.
3. Flips through book stopping at some colour photographs.
4. Comes upon bold heading 'Magpies' starts to read first few lines of text — loses interest.
5. Goes back to the beginning of the book but ignores or is not aware of contents page. Starts to read from the beginning — an introductory section about encouraging birds to come into the garden.
6. Turns over to next page — studies illustrations but not caption — begins to read from the top about birds migrating.

Comment

If children are going to learn to operate successfully in informational reading it is important that they have questions needing an answer in their mind or jotted down; this is the starting point.

Starting with a query they need first to consult the contents and index pages. They need to know the purpose and arrangement of these sections. For the index page they need to have familiarity with alphabetical order and with the spelling of the word they are looking for. More important than these mechanical skills they will need to understand the concept of key words and cross references. Children will also need to be able to scan down these pages without reading every word closely. We are already describing some quite complex skills and most children need considerable help with this. The most useful resource is a set of information books for the teacher and a group of children to work on together. For scanning individual pages of text the OHP is very useful. Discussion, demonstration, trying it out and feedback are needed. For most children the process of internalizing effective strategies is a gradual one needing a good deal of experience, encouragement and guidance.

A Focus on Writing

Writing serves two purposes for us. Through writing we can communicate with people over place and time. We can also use writing for our own learning, to note down our study and research and to clarify our thinking for ourselves.

As in reading younger junior children need guidance, encouragement and opportunity to widen their writing repertoire and to go more deeply into the writing process. In the infant school children will have encountered personal, expressive and narrative writing together with straightforward accounts and reports usually ordered chronologically. They may have also written letters, messages, labels and brief instructions. These kinds of writing need to continue and be refined, added to these there will perhaps be a start in persuasive writing with some children beginning discursive writing — putting forward an argument from different points of view.

This section will look at:

different types of writing;
readers for children's writing;
working with the writing process;
practical aspects of organization.

Types of Writing

Suggested observation task
Collect a 'typical' child's writing over a week through all areas of the curriculum.

For each example note down the situation in which the writing occurred, the purpose of the writing and the intended reader(s) for the writing.

Comment

You should notice that different kinds of writing for different purposes and different intended readers are already emerging. The style of the writing should be starting to reflect:

(i) the nature of the activity it accompanies, (for example, charting results so as to be able to contribute to a final report of an experiment) and;

(ii) the intended reader, (for example, a story written for friends' interest and enjoyment).

How Can We Help Children to Widen the Range of Their Writing?

Some of the ways in which we can do this are as follows:

1. Giving children opportunities through varied activities and 'real' purposes together with 'real' readers. Given a purposeful context for writing children are much more likely to be fully engaged in their writing task. Writing to practice writing with no end purpose rarely engages children.

2. Giving children examples of different kinds of writing. These examples can come from around the classroom or from texts of various kinds. Reading from these kinds of texts to children and commenting on the kind of writing used will start to make children more aware. Children who are increasingly making use of information texts will start to 'pick up' the various kinds of writing, but this process, cannot be relied upon solely.

3. By demonstration and discussion. As teachers with younger and less experienced writers write for and with them in an apprenticeship approach, so they can write for and with older children with the focus on the appropriate style of writing. Using the OHP or large sheets of paper the teacher can write for and with a group of children drawing attention while writing to significant features in the writing and, perhaps, contrasting and comparing with other kinds of writing that children are familiar with.

4. By discussion and feedback. When children have been attempting various kinds of writing teachers can give children feedback on this (usually in groups with, perhaps, one child's writing as a focus)

and discuss how effective the writing has been in its clarity and for its purpose and intended reader.

Readers for Children's Writing

Looking back at the examples of children's writing over a week or thinking about your own writing over the last week, you will be able to state who the intended reader was for each piece of writing.

Having a reader in mind while writing helps us and children to develop a clarity and an appropriate style to make the reading easier. This is a gradual process of development and will go on well into the upper junior stage and beyond into secondary school. The awareness of a reader and the reader's needs develop partly as a result of social and cognitive growth and partly as a result of the situation in which the writing is accomplished.

It is very difficult for children to begin to develop appropriate styles of writing when the only reader for their writing is the teacher who 'knows it all' anyway, the task can then become perfunctory. If the purpose is to inform people who do not know then children are obliged to grapple with the style of writing as well as the content in order to get the message across.

Suggested task

Listed below are the possible readers for children's writing. Try to think of instances of the kinds of writing that children might attempt for each group of readers.

Self
Peers
Wider known readership
Wider unknown readership

Example

Writing for self

The kinds of writing that would be mainly for the child's own reading would be 'diary' writing, news writing, writing a commentary in a 'journal', plans for writing, notes from reading, listening or for working something out.

Writing for peers

This could include stories, poems, accounts, reports, charts and diagrams, informing those who don't already know, messages and notes.

Writing for a wider, known readership

Stories and poems for younger children might feature here as well as notices for the school, captions for display outside the classroom, letters to the head, other teachers, parents.

Writing for a wider, unknown readership

This might include writing letters for information, advertising school events, and writing to authors.

Comment

A successful example of children's writing to an outside unknown reader was as follows. The local branch library was being threatened with closure. It was decided to write to local councillors to try to stop this threatened closure. After class talk children drafted, proof read and rewrote their letters. Instances of likely hardship were given in the letters; old people and young families who would find it difficult to get to the central library. All the letters were sent with a covering letter from the teacher. A while later a councillor replied on behalf of a committee who had decided to reconsider the situation. The letter told the children that their letters had influenced the decision!

Working With the Writing Process

Suggested self-observation task
When you are engaged in a finished piece of writing (say, an essay) for someone to read, what stages do you go through in the process of writing?

Try to list these stages down in the order which they occur.

Example

In writing this particular chapter there were many stages to be gone through before the final product that you are now reading. Individual writers may vary in the stages they go through, but overall there is a pattern that emerges. The particular stages that marked the production of this chapter were as follows:

    (i) *Germination of idea*, thinking there is a need for this kind of book.

    (ii) *Talking with others*, discussing the idea at a very early stage with co-writers and publishers.

    (iii) *Devising an outline plan*, the shape and the important points of style and content — this was done in collaboration — deciding who would write which section.

    (iv) *Brainstorming*, using a web diagram noting down everything that was important to include.

    (v) *Writing an outline plan* with headings in the form of a flow diagram.

    (vi) *Checking* back with co-writers at this stage.

    (vii) *Beginning a first draft*, writing some parts in some detail using the outline plan — some parts with brief headings or key words.

    (viii) *Reading and revising* first draft.

    (ix) *Writing up a second draft*, cutting up parts of the first draft to use without alteration.

    (x) *Reading and revising* the second draft.

    (xi) *Final draft* for co-writer to consider — still a few gaps evident where examples are needed or where relevant information is not easily accessible.

    (xii) *Final modifications* on advice of co-writer filling in last remaining gaps.

    (xiii) *Manuscript goes to publisher*, read by copy editor.

    (xiv) Suggested minor changes accepted or rejected.

    (xv) *Page proofs printed*, proofs sent back to writers.

    (xvi) *Final proof reading*

In between all these stages time elapsed and other aspects of work were attended to. It is important that this happens, it enables the writer to see the writing afresh and also enables thinking processes to go on subconsciously so that new ideas or new ways of expressing are thrown up.

During the time of writing, various books were read, many conversations with students, teachers and advisors took place, all influencing the course of the writing.

The use of the word processor does streamline and accelerate the writing process.

Comment

Of course the writing of this chapter is not typical of the usual kind of writing we do. Often we write mainly for ourselves, study notes, lists, reminders etc. or the kind of writing that would only need a brief proof-reading: friendly letters, messages, simple form-filling. For some of the writing that children engage in they need opportunity and guidance to work with the writing process rather than do 'one draft' writing that is handed in to the teacher for some kind of response. Narrative and poetry writing are examples of this as is informational writing as a result of project study.

In all writing that needs more than one draft, the stages just described overlap and merge, for instance, the outline plan is formulated early on, but this is changed and added to in later stages.

Younger junior children are beginning to be able and willing to work on some of their pieces of writing in order to refine them and get their voice across more clearly. Some children at this age still find the effort of writing so laborious that any drafting would probably be through discussion only, though, of course, they would be able to contribute to discussions leading to other children's rewriting.

For younger writers to go through the writing process with some of their pieces they need the following:

(a) The opportunity, time, resources and classroom organization that back up the process.

(b) 'Ownership' of their writing — a strong urge to write that particular piece and a strong interest in getting the message across to groups of readers.

(c) A chance to make choices about topics for writing.

(d) A chance to discuss the writing while it is in process, with teacher and/or friends in order to receive feedback.

(e) Help in developing aspects of their writing at a point where they can benefit from it.

Children Proof-reading Their Writing

When children have made the content, style and organization of their writing as good as they can at that moment the piece will need proof-reading. Going over a piece looking for errors in spelling and punctuation can be difficult, especially directly after a piece of writing is completed. We often do not notice our original errors. To help children in this necessary task the following points can be helpful:

(a) leave some time before they go back to the writing;
(b) read it softly aloud to themselves — this helps to mark the sentences;
(c) exchange the writing with a friend and proof-reading each other's work. It is often easier to notice errors in someone else's work;
(d) use a dictionary for some of the spelling miscues that they have underlined when drafting.

When the child has done as much of this work as possible then the teacher needs to offer direct help. Help is best given alongside the child. The learning is taking place in the context of the child's own writing intentions. The teacher has to use a fine judgment in deciding when to correct with a brief comment, when to make a teaching point and when to ask the child to make further efforts. It is important always to be encouraging and praise what has gone well. Many teachers jot down points of growth so that they can become part of the child's writing record and also so that she/he can draw together groups of children who have similar needs.

Spelling

Learning to spell correctly is a gradual process and involves training the visual memory. Some teaching principles to follow at this point might be:

(a) helping children to spell correctly words that they need frequently in their writing;
(b) using children's writing as the context for working on spelling;
(c) always asking children to rewrite the whole word that needs to be corrected;
(d) trying to show children patterns within and between words, giving them the 'hooks' of familiar words to 'hang' new words onto;
(e) when children are using word banks or dictionaries

    — asking them never to just copy always to look carefully — cover — write and then check;

(f) when showing children correct spellings — to always write them — never say them — and to draw attention to the salient part(s) of the word while writing.

(g) taking time out to play word games, drawing attention to spelling on captions around the room, print in the environment.

It is important that children are willing to take risks, experiment and hypothesize with spelling. This is the way we learn. Good spelling is an important social skill. Poor or careless spelling in an adult is embarrassing and can give a false impression of capability. Before the introduction of the printing press quite scholarly people used to spell in a variety of ways and this was acceptable as long as the meaning was clear.

If children get too anxious about spelling correctly they will find it difficult to learn and to train their visual memory. They will also become inhibited in their written expression, unwilling to use words that they might misspell.

Punctuation

Punctuation is an abstract concept concerned with making writing available to a reader across time and space. Learning how to punctuate correctly develops gradually — more effort is made at learning when the child has a stake in the writing and when a reader is identified for the writing.

Reading the writing aloud to themselves, with a teacher or more experienced writer, helps children to identify the sentence units as does proof-reading someone else's writing. Individual work on a piece of writing for publication with the teacher is invaluable. Often teachers can demonstrate points of punctuation when they write for a class. Reading print in the classroom as well as in books and other materials also helps children to come to an understanding of punctuation. The understanding is accelerated when attention is drawn to the punctuation.

An example of a clear illustration of the question mark is on the questioning captions that teachers often place on displays — 'How tall are the bean plants now?' 'How many children had *Neighbours* for their favourite TV programme?'

Handwriting

Traditionally, younger junior children may at this stage be coming to grips with cursive handwriting. Usually the whole school adopts the same style. Some infant schools are now starting children off in a cursive style as it saves them relearning a new style later. It is also felt that joining letters can help to establish spelling patterns in the visual memory.

The ultimate aim for handwriting is that it is flowing, easy and legible. If a piece of writing is destined in its final draft to be read by readers other than the teacher then the writer has more reason to attend to the handwriting.

Despite the fact that an increasing number of infant schools are taking up cursive writing in the early stages of children's writing, the first year or so in the junior school is still often the time for 'joining up'. There are several teachers' books together with work books that deal with this, taking the teacher and children through well defined steps. The school will almost certainly have a whole school approach to the teaching of handwriting.

Essentially it is the movement of the hand and writing tool that is important. Patterns and letter formation practice must emphasize the correct movement which enables an economical and uninterrupted flow to the writing.

Handwriting sessions need to be short, intensive and regular at this stage. A good context for careful writing using the skills learnt is in compiling an anthology of favourite short poems. Actual practice of joining letters needs to be carefully supervised to see that children are using the correct movements. The 'odd moment' practice with practice cards is questionable as children do not always go about the task in the required way. They may well be reinforcing movements which will inhibit the flow of their writing.

When the teacher is demonstrating writing for the class it is essential that the children can see the movement of the hand clearly. Above all the sessions should be enjoyable with a good deal of encouragement and praise for effort offered by the teacher.

Practical Arrangements for Writing in the Classroom

Schools and classrooms are not always the best places to write in! Think of yourself as a writer — where do you like to write, do you have a special place? What do you need to start you off? A coffee

— a brisk walk beforehand? Do you write best in silence or with music (we very seldom write well with voices in the background — we want to listen in). What is the best time of day (or night) for you as a writer? Can you overcome unfavourable circumstances if you persevere or is it better for you to postpone the writing until another time? For some kinds of writing, notably imaginative and expressive writing we are not always 'in the mood'.

When teachers have classes of more then thirty children they cannot reproduce ideal writing conditions for each child! Children gain tremendously from being part of a writing community — from working and talking together as well as being an individual writer. Inevitably though there are many times when the world shrinks to a writer, the pen and the page.

Time

Wherever possible children need some choice over the order of their learning tasks, giving some limited flexibility over when to get down to that intensive piece of writing.

Children need time to think and reflect for initial ideas to germinate. If the topic for writing is going to be given by the teacher it is a good idea to introduce it and have an initial discussion before the item for the main concentrated effort of writing.

We all compose and transcribe at different rates — this can often depend upon the nature of the writing and the 'inspiration' that goes with it. Arrangements need to be made for children to go as far as they can with a piece of writing.

Organization

Here again, thoughtfulness and flexibility are the keys. Sometimes it is good for a whole class to write together at the same time. Stimulus and ideas can be discussed. Brainstorming and wordstorming are made available to everyone, an urgency is generated, people spark each other off. At other times it is difficult for the teacher to offer help and support if the whole class are at the same stage of 'intensive' writing at the same time. Here some children could be directed towards other activities or might be encouraged to concentrate on illustrations for example.

Materials

All the materials for writing need to be readily available. Writing folders can be more flexible than exercise books. Children might be encouraged to use felt tips and coloured paper in their first draft writing. This helps to reinforce the idea that at this stage the writing can be 'played around with'. Scissors need to be available for cutting up the writing and reorganizing it.

Pencils are not the easiest writing tools — they vary in length as they wear down and are either blunt or sharp and can break just when an intensive phase of writing is in progress! Fibre-tips or biros or whatever flows smoothly and is legible is best.

Choice of size and shape of paper for a published piece of writing is important. It is another factor in demonstrating ownership and the value of the individual child's voice in the writing.

Environment

Environment can imply the physical surroundings and also the atmosphere generated in a class or school. It is important to create an atmosphere where writing is treated seriously and children seen as apprentices in the craft of writing. Children's writing should be well displayed, their books alongside others in the reading corner. Other writing such as reports, instructions, posters, queries, notices should be sited in accessible places and should be drawn attention to. Sometimes teachers should read the writing to the whole class at their story time.

It cannot be overemphasized that children need to see teachers writing. Teachers write notes and comments to children, can contribute to their journals, share their own writing efforts with the children, make a child aware of internal and external correspondence dealing with the affairs of the school.

Physically there needs to be a place in the classroom for free writing. As in the infant classroom children need a corner set up for writing where two or three can write as they like at free choice activity times. Ideally a word processor or a typewriter might be in the corner together with all the necessary materials for writing.

Recording, Monitoring and Assessing Children's Writing

Most of the opportunities to record comments on children's writing come from the discussions between teacher and child over a piece of ongoing writing.

Careful and detailed record-keeping is necessary for monitoring progress and assessing children's next learning points. Records must also be kept in order to communicate the stage of the child's development to the child, parents, other teachers and possibly to support agencies.

Suggested task

Here is a piece of writing from an 7-year-old girl, Ann. She wrote this alliterative poem after the whole class had discussed alliteration and had done a word storm. Together they had combined to write the first two lines with the teacher. Each child had then been encouraged to write their own piece, this was the first draft that Ann produced.

one wiggly warm wonder
in the water.

X two tiered toads tidy up
the tangerines.

Three thirsty thrushes thought
about thieving.

X four Fencing frogs flew
five flies

Five fearless fences
fight four fat flies.

Six sad sealions sitting
in the sea

Seven seeing seahorses
sit on the seat

eight eabing ealseat
eight Seals

nine neat nuts need
needling up

Ten Teaching Teachers
Teach Tangerines

The children were encouraged to see writing as a game with rules at this stage. They were encouraged not to spend too much time worrying over spellings. They chose what to write with and what colour sugar paper to write on. They had to write as much as they could in five minutes.

Ann read the poem aloud as she wrote it and kept going back to read it from the beginning. All the children were encouraged to do this, particularly in this type of poem where sound was crucial. With other types of poems reading aloud had helped a good deal in developing their sense of rhythm.

What points would you note down as a teacher regarding this piece?

These are some which might be noted:

Intentions. Were they met?
Yes, generally the rules were kept to. The teacher's intention that the writing should be light hearted and enjoyed without the pressure of 'getting things right' was certainly met.

Content, originality
The children had been encouraged to think of unusual juxtapositions of adjectives and nouns. Ann has done this, particularly with 'four fencing frogs' and 'nine neat nuts'. The poem might have had more impact if the topic of creatures had been sustained throughout.

Organization
This was already laid down from the rules of the poetry game and did not require much thought in this instance.

Choice and variety of vocabulary
The framework had been given to the children, but within this Ann managed very well — although line 5 does not seem to sound right and 'tangerines' come into lines 2 and 10.
(Teaching point: The class did not have access to good clear dictionaries. These would almost certainly have helped in producing this kind of poem.)

Style
This was already modelled in the word-storm, discussion and example two lines at the beginning of the poem.

Spelling
This looks competent. There are two errors and 'tiered' was copied incorrectly from the blackboard, but overall there is a high degree of accuracy.

Punctuation
Some lines begin with capital letters but not all. This could be a worthwhile teaching point to pursue. Some lines do not have full stops. This could be because of the pace of the writing.

Handwriting
As this was a 'fun' first draft it would be inappropriate to criticize this too much, although it is generally legible.

Appearance/format/presentation
Ann may like to keep the lines between each line of the poem, otherwise there is little to say on this point as this is first draft writing.

Teachers often have a book for noting down dated comments to themselves for future teaching guidance. For example, 'Brian's writing is full of ands and theirs, must get a group together to focus on this'. 'Emma always has difficulty at the start of a piece of writing — will have a brainstorming session on this'.

More formal records that would be communicated to other people might well be compiled at certain points during the year or at the end of an academic year. To enable a true profile to be compiled — pieces of children's writing throughout the year need to be collected and stored. They need to be dated and to have brief notes of the context for the writing — how it was accomplished, what support was offered, whether it went beyond one draft. Specific points of compositional and secretarial aspects can be made. The teacher has then a basis on which to judge the child's development as a writer.

Whatever the form of recording adopted it needs to be part of a coherent whole-school policy. Records need to be informative and useful, but at the same time must not be over-elaborate and time consuming. This is easier said than done!

Talking and Listening

Talking has had very little specific mention in this chapter, though the need for and the functions of talk have been implied throughout. Talk is the main means of transacting the learning, the social relationships and the organization within a classroom community. Most acts of literacy are surrounded by talk. In a piece of writing the ideas are discussed and the piece is planned through talk. After the piece is completed it is commented on by writer, teacher and friends and future development may be discussed. The same kind of interaction of the four modes of language might take place around an act of reading.

When children and teachers are working on a project, talk, 'cements' the processes and activities that are developed towards a final outcome.

The kinds of talk that are developed through project work might look like this:

Teacher and Whole Class

Introduction to project.

Discussion — what do you already know?

Negotiating areas of enquiry and parameters of project.

Negotiating subdivision of topic into different aspects.

Negotiating working groups.

Discussing different forms of final product and intended readers/audience.

Within Working Groups

Children plan and discuss with and without the teacher — agreeing tasks, informing, directing, explaining, establishing, negotiating, confirming, denying.

Between Working Groups and Teachers

Questioning and answering.
Reporting back to teacher.
Negotiating form of final outcome.

Between Working Groups and Rest of Class

Interim working reports.
Questioning other groups.
Answering other children's questions.
Evaluating theirs and other groups' work and presentations.

Between Class and 'Visitors'

Asking prepared questions.
Asking more probing questions following initial enquiry.
(Sometimes tape-recordings are made of interviews — transcripts and reports from these would have to be discussed.)

Between Class and Audience

A formal presentation to rest of school in assembly.
Explaining to children in another class.
Explaining to parents/governors/head/other teachers.

Concluding Comments

This stage of children's developing literacy is not unique within the overall pattern of development — it is part of the continuum. Some children between 7 and 9 will be operating at the stage of most children in the final year of infant school, some will be functioning more like children in the upper junior school. Each stage is built upon earlier experiences and provides the foundations for later ones.

Traditionally we think of the infant stage as providing a firm foundation on which the children's literacy can be widened and their understanding of the literacy processes deepened. This process of widening the range of reading and writing and increasing the depth of understanding of literacy belongs in this early junior stage.

Chapter 6

Literacy in the Later Junior Years

Introduction

This chapter is specifically concerned with the literacy opportunities and demands of the later years in the junior school. It is important, however, that it is seen in conjunction with the previous chapters, especially that relating to the early junior years. Children's experience of literacy in school should be seen as a continuous process, rather than one of differentiated stages, and many of the points which will be made in this chapter will echo previous chapters.

It is also the case, of course, that at any stage in the education process children will be operating at a variety of levels. The 'typical' upper junior child is a rarity. It is worthwhile exploring some of this variability between children before we proceed with the main body of this chapter.

Suggestion for observation
Choose two children at random from a class with whom you have contact. Using any strategies which seem appropriate, attempt to make assessments, over a period of days, of both these children's abilities in the following areas:

> fluency in reading aloud;
> understanding of reading;
> ability to use books etc. to find information;
> breadth of vocabulary in writing;
> ability to write cogently about a topic;
> technical writing ability (spelling, handwriting etc.).

Points to consider
There is a slight chance that you will have happened to pick upon

two children with very similar characteristics, but it is far more likely that you will have noticed some differences between these children. These differences are likely to be of two kinds. You probably found differences between the children on several of the dimensions mentioned above. Children do vary in their abilities to perform in literacy tasks. You are also likely to have found differences in individual children's abilities across the dimensions of literacy. You may have found that, for example:

> being able to read aloud fluently did not necessarily imply good understanding of what was read;

> being able to write interesting and thoughtful pieces did not always go with good spelling and neat handwriting;

and other similar discrepancies. Children's literacy development is invariably patchy.

Comment

Given this variability, both between different children's abilities in the various dimensions of literacy, and between individuals' mastery of these dimensions, the task of the teacher becomes quite taxing. The teacher has to:

> ensure that each child gets appropriate experience and teaching in literacy, which implies a curriculum which can cater for individual needs;

> beware of assuming that because children can perform well (or badly) in one dimension of literacy they will necessarily perform well (or badly) in others.

Throughout the rest of this chapter, you will need to bear in mind this variability. In thinking about the 'upper junior child', it is almost impossible not to think in terms of an average. Remember, though, that the 'average' child is a statistical construction rather than a reality.

The above points notwithstanding, it is possible to examine the main tasks in upper junior classes in terms of the major aims for literacy which teachers may have. This chapter will spend some time examining two general aims:

(a) that of extending the range of interactions which children have with literacy;

(b) that of deepening their involvement in literate experiences and increasing their stamina.

Extending the Range of Interactions with Literacy

Before exploring how children's experiences might be extended, we need to look at the current range of their experiences, both in reading and writing.

Suggested activity — A literacy survey
Over a period of at least a week make a survey of the reading and writing experiences of a group of children. You might keep the survey yourself, or you might involve the children by asking them to keep reading and writing diaries. For each piece of reading and writing done try to get answers to these questions:

Why was this being done?
What format of material was being dealt with?

At the end of the period, try to summarize your results. What implications do these have?

Comments: Reading

The issue of format was mentioned in Chapter 1, and at that point it was suggested that because adults have to read a wide variety of formats of texts, then children should be given experience across this range. In Chapter 1 the following, non-exhaustive list of formats was given:

books	brochures
stories	advertisements
poems	pamphlets
newspapers	forms
letters	timetables
graphs	instructions
diagrams	maps
magazines	computer screens
notes	posters

It is unlikely that you found this diversity of range in your survey. You might like to compare the range you did find with that found by a student who surveyed the reading experience of twelve third year juniors over a week. Her figures were as follows:

	%
worksheets/workbooks	43

books	21
blackboard	19
comics	9
computer screen	3
computer printout	1

It seems likely that many children experience a narrow range of formats in their reading, the predominance of which is of a very specialized kind. Few adults read workbooks.

With regard to purposes for reading, you may have found it difficult to classify your results. Much of the reading children do in school is done in order to do something else, as these examples from the student's survey show.

'I read this bit so I could answer this question',
'I read this so I could fill in the box',
'I read the blackboard so I could copy the word down'.

A possible classification system was suggested in Chapter 1, namely:

(i) reading to get information;
(ii) reading for pleasure;
(iii) reading to get better at reading.

These purposes may, of course, overlap. It was suggested in Chapter 1 that children reading simply for the third of these purposes was perhaps more commonly the case than it need be. Certainly by the time children reach top junior level we might hope that the balance of their purposes for reading would have shifted to the first two in this list.

Notice, however, that a greal deal of children's experience of reading tends to be rather vague in terms of purpose. Each of the three children's statements above invite the question, 'Why?' The children's ultimate purpose may simply be, 'Because teacher told me.' We certainly need to consider how we can make children's purposes for reading real ones.

Comments: Writing

As an indication of the type of balance which you might have found, compare the findings of the fourteen class teachers in a junior school who were asked to keep diaries for a period of a month of all the writing they asked their children to do. This writing was analyzed into types using very broad categories and the percentage of each type of writing is given below in descending order of frequency.

	%
Narrative	51
Poetry	12
Descriptive	10
Reporting	7
Personal	6
Letters	5
Recording	5
Instructions	2
Note-taking	2

Clearly there are some problems of precise definitions here, but the table makes revealing reading. The absolute priority of narrative (stories) is clear and will probably be recognized by most primary teachers. The low emphasis placed upon information based writing will also be recognized as fairly common. The absence of forms of writing such as notices, advertisements and arguments will likewise cause little surprise. It is fairly clear that the balance here is heavily biased towards one form of writing, and that, if this picture is reflective of practice at large, there needs to be some attention to correcting this imbalance.

The classification of purposes for writing has been attempted by many people, with greater or lesser clarity. One classification model which has become popular and is extremely useful is that suggested by Beard (1983) and based upon the model of communication put forward by Kinneavy (1971).

Kinneavy characterizes communication as taking place within a context with three major reference points, each of which form one point of a triangle, the message or content of the communication being in the centre.

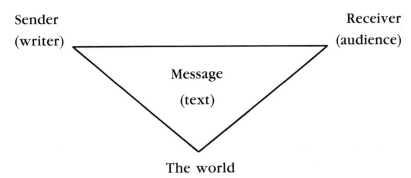

Sender (writer)

Receiver (audience)

Message (text)

The world

The model, of course, applies equally to forms of communication beyond writing.

Beard suggests that a classification of writing according to purpose might be arrived at by focusing in turn on each of the four elements of the model. Thus writing which is chiefly done with the needs of the writer in mind might be said to have expressive aims; that is, be attempting to clarify ideas and feelings in the writer himself.

Similarly writing focused on its audience will have the aim of influencing that audience to some degree and might be said to have persuasive aims. Writing which refers very powerfully to the world at large can be said to have referential aims. Finally, writing which focuses specifically on the shape of the text itself might be said to have literary aims.

Obviously there will be a great deal of overlap within any individual piece of writing. A poem, for example, might have expressive aims for its author as it is a vehicle for the expression of deep feelings, but it will also have literary aims, being written in a very particular form which makes its own demands. Nevertheless there are certain forms of writing which seem to fit naturally into either of the four categories given by the model, and it seems a very useful model to take as a basis for ensuring a range of writing experiences. We can list forms of writing under each of the four categories.

Writing With Expressive Aims
Diaries, news, anecdote and narrative, personal writing

Writing With Literary Aims
Stories, poetry, jokes and riddles

Writing With Persuasive Aims
Advertisements, letters, arguments

Writing With Referential Aims
Reports, notices, instructions, questionnaires, notes, information leaflets, explanations.

Extending Stamina and Involvement

It is fairly logical to assume that the older children get the more they should be able to sustain interactions with texts, whether reading or writing. Their concentration span should lengthen and with it their reading and writing stamina. The depth to which children become involved in reading and writing need not necessarily alter. Even very young children can, if the conditions are right, get extremely involved in these tasks. Anyone who has watched a 5-year-old struggle to write her name, or get absorbed in an exciting picture book, can testify that young children are as likely to become fully absorbed in literate behaviour as older ones. Yet the increasing concentration span of older children should make us expect them to show this absorption in literacy as a regular event. The available evidence would, however, suggest that this does not happen.

The best evidence comes from the work of Lunzer and Gardner (1979), who carried out observations of fifty hours lessons in top junior classes. They found that the vast majority of these pupils' reading experience was made up of short bursts of reading of less than thirty seconds in duration, with at best only 13 per cent of the reading done being more sustained than one minute.

You might like to observe some children reading to see exactly what they do.

Suggestion for observation
Choose two 10 or 11-year-old children at random and observe them during the course of a school lesson. (You will probably find it difficult to keep up this kind of sustained observation for longer than an hour at a time.) Note down the times at which the children do any reading, and any times at which this is interrupted or they go on to do something else.

At the end of the lesson, try to work out how much time these children have spent actually reading, and how long the longest period was. If this pattern were to continue during the whole day, how much experience of continuous involvement in reading would these children have received?

An example
The following extract is taken from a teacher's observation notes and describes one period of 'reading' experience for a 10-year-old boy.

Time	Activity
11.10	Opens textbook
11.11	Picks pencil off floor
11.12	Goes to sharpen pencil
11.20	Returns to desk

11.23	Looks at open textbook for approximately twenty seconds, then writes a title in exercise book
11.26	Looks around room
11.28	Looks at textbook [thirty seconds]
11.29	Writes in exercise book
11.33	Rubs out word
11.37	Rewrites word
11.40	Looks in textbook [forty-five seconds]
11.41	Asks neighbour a question
11.42	Writes in exercise book
11.44	Opens desk, takes out ruler
11.45	Writes in exercise book
11.47	Looks in textbook [thirty seconds]
11.48	Looks at blackboard
11.50	Writes in exercise book
11.53	Looks in textbook [thirty seconds]
11.54	Writes in exercise book
11.57	Takes book to show teacher. She praises him for a much better effort
12.00	Returns to seat. Closes book

Comments

During this forty-minute period (marked on the teacher's timetable as a reading lesson) this child actually read for a total of less than three minutes, with the longest sustained burst being of forty-five seconds duration. He wrote for approximately eighteen minutes which produced two one-word answers and two short sentences. At no time during the lesson did the teacher admonish him for not working, which suggests his behaviour was not specially lazy. Indeed, the fact that she praised him at the end suggest that other occasions he may well have worked less conscientiously.

Of course, one extract does not prove the case. This may have been an exceptional day, or an exceptional child. Compare it with the results of your own close observations. To really put this to the test, the best way is to deliberately choose, say, a half-hour period when you are certain a particular child will read concentratedly, and observe this period very carefully, noting down exactly what the child does. This will give you the best possible picture against which to judge your other observations.

If the points made above are even partially accurate, it does suggest that sustained involvement with text is comparatively rare in the junior classroom. This is clearly unsatisfactory, and some of the activities described later in this chapter have the explicit purpose of encouraging greater and longer involvement. For the moment, we can examine briefly some of the underlying factors which might give rise to this more sustained involvement.

The key to getting children to be more involved with texts can be stated in one word: motivation. All of us know that we concentrate harder on tasks if we can see clearly why we are doing them, and if they are important to us, and children are no exception. It was suggested earlier that for much of children's literate behaviour in schools, the only real reason they have for doing it is because 'teacher said so'. If this is the case, their lack of real involvement is perhaps not surprising.

To engender motivation, leading to greater involvement, we need to try to ensure either of two things. Either children need to be genuinely interested in the activity they are doing, or they need to see it as an essential step towards an end-product they really value. Unfortunately a great many of the reading and writing activities children are asked to do in school are not in themselves particularly interesting and neither is it often clear what their end product is.

This chapter so far has examined the major literacy aims for this stage of schooling, and has suggested that many traditional teaching practices and activities do not actually help achieve these aims. The rest of the chapter will present a more positive picture by examining strategies and techniques the teacher can employ to increase the likelihood of success in these aims.

The Centrality of Oracy

The point has already been made several times in this book that talk underpins and supports the development of literacy in fundamental ways. Talk can also be used with deliberate teaching purposes as a way of encouraging deeper involvement with reading tasks. You might try the following two activities in order to see this clearly.

Suggestion for observation: 1
Give a group of three or four children a cloze text to complete. Explain that there may be several possible answers for each deletion, but that they have to agree entirely amongst themselves before filling in the

deletions. Tape record their discussion if possible. (If not you will have to eavesdrop, but by doing this you are likely to affect their discussion very severely.)

Points to consider
This activity forces the children to discuss and come to agreement. Listen carefully to their discussion and pick out any points at which you think one or other of them seems actually to be learning. This may show itself as:

> a child accepting someone else's suggestion;
> a child trying to explain his own ideas to another;
> children coming to a joint decision;
> a child having an idea sparked off by someone else's.

Would you class this as a useful activity for these children?

Suggestion for observation: 2
Use a reading comprehension exercise, preferably an interesting one. Instead of asking children to write down answers to the questions individually, arrange them into groups of maximum four children. Give each group two questions only to answer and allow them time to discuss their answers thoroughly. Ask them to write only after this discussion is finished.

Points to consider
Can you detect any increase in the level of thinking about the text? Is this reflected in the kind of answers they produce?

Comment

The activity with the comprehension exercise was done by a teacher of 12-year-olds (see Wray *et al*, 1989). He used the same exercise with another class but in the traditonal way, with children answering questions individually. He noticed that the children who had had opportunities to discuss questions wrote, on average, answers four times as long, and showing a commensurate increase in depth of thought. They were also much more enthusiastic about the activity.

What is it about talk which produces this depth of involvement in the reading activity?

Firstly it is possible to be much more tentative in expressing ideas in talk than in writing. Ideas written down achieve an instant permanence which they may not merit, and this can, therefore, deter tentative exploration. In discussion, however, one can make it clear that ideas are only tentative. Hesitations, false starts, changes of direction, expressions such as 'er', 'I think', 'probably' all have this effect. Ideas are thus open to comment, elaboration or rejection by others in non-threatening ways.

A second feature of talk is its shared nature. In discussion it is not incumbent upon one person to come up with all the ideas and work them through all alone. The group shares this task, and take up each others' ideas, and learn by doing so. In group discussion the whole is definitely more than the sum of the parts.

A final feature of group talk which you probably noticed quite frequently is the way in which participants regularly bring in personal experiences and anecdotes. These may, to an outsider, often seem like red-herrings, but almost always they have the function of linking previous experience with the new ideas being discussed. This 'anchoring' of new ideas has a marked learning benefit; indeed, learning is actually impossible without it. Group talk deepens learning and helps participants make new ideas their own.

Reading and Writing to Learn

The important role which discussion can play in deepening understanding of reading should be borne in mind during this section, when we examine the important issue of learning through reading and writing.

Most teachers of junior children will see a large part of their role in developing reading as being concerned with developing children's abilities to understand and learn from written materials. Activities to develop this have traditionally occupied a large part of reading instruction at the top junior level. Chief amongst these activities has been the 'comprehension exercise', which usually consists of a passage of text followed by several questions which readers have to answer. To get a flavour of the activity you might like to try the following:

Activity
Read the following passage:

> The chanks vos blunging frewly bedeng the brudegan. Some chanks vos unred but the other chanks vos unredder. They vos all polet and rather chiglop so they did not mekle the spuler. A few were unstametick.

Now write down to answers to the following questions:

   (i) What were the chanks doing?
  (ii) How well did they blunge?
 (iii) Where were they blunging?
  (iv) In what ways were the chanks the same?
   (v) In what ways were they different?
  (vi) Were any chanks stametick?

Comment

You should have found it comparatively easy to find the answers to these questions. You have therefore successfully completed a comprehension exercise (designed to develop your understanding of your reading) without actually understanding any of the text! How did this happen?

What in fact you rely on to complete exercises like this is your intuitive knowledge of how the language system works. You know, for instance, that questions which begin 'How well did . . .?' expect adverbs as an answer, which, you know, in English usually end in 'ly'. You know that one of the functions of prefixes is to make words mean the opposite, so you reasoned that the opposite of 'unstametick' was probably 'stametick', and answered accordingly. You can do all this without actually understanding what these words mean, and if you can do this, then probably children can do the same when they complete their comprehension exercises. This suggests that to develop real understanding, we need to choose alternative activities.

Before looking at some of these activities we need to look at what the understanding of texts rests upon. To begin to examine this, read the following passage a couple of times, then close the book and try to write down what you remember of it.

Ilya Prigogine has demonstrated that when an 'open system', one which exchanges matter and/or energy with its environment, has reached a state of maximum entropy, its molecules are in a state of equilibirum. Spontaneously, small fluctuations can increase in amplitude, bringing the system into a 'far from equilibrium' state. Perhaps it is the instability of sub-atomic particles (events) on the microscopic level that causes fluctuations on the so-called macroscopic level of molecules. At any rate, strongly fluctuating molecules in a far-from-equilibrium state are highly unstable. Responding to internal and/or external influences, they may either degenerate into chaos or reorganise at a higher level of complexity. (from Weaver, 1988)

You probably found it difficult to remember much of this passage for the simple reason that it makes little sense to you. What is it that makes it difficult?

People commonly attribute difficulty in understanding texts to the difficult words used. This passage certainly has many obscure words which do cause difficulty. Understanding, however, relies on something a good deal deeper than just knowledge of vocabulary. To see this, read the following passage and try to make sense of it.

> The procedure is actually quite simple. First you arrange things into different groups. Of course one pile may be sufficient depending on how much there is to do. If you have to go somewhere else due to lack of facilities that is the next step, otherwise you are pretty well set. It is important not to overdo things. That is, it is better to do too few things at once than too many. In the short run this may not seem important but complications can easily arise. A mistake can be expensive as well. At first the whole procedure will seem complicated. Soon however, it will become just another facet of life. It is difficult to foresee any end to the necessity for this task in the immediate future, but then one can never tell. After the procedure is completed one arranges the materials into different groups again. Then they can be put into their appropriate places. Eventually they will be used once more and the whole cycle will then have to be repeated. However, that is a part of life. (from Bransford and Johnson, 1973)

In this passage there are no difficult words, yet it is still very hard to understand. However, once you are told that the passage describes the procedure for washing clothes, you can understand it perfectly easily.

What really makes the difference in understanding text is the background knowledge of the reader. If you have adequate previous knowledge, and if you realize which particular knowledge the new passage links with, then understanding can take place. This background knowledge can be thought of in terms of structures of ideas, or schemata (Rumelhart, 1984). Understanding becomes the process of fitting new information into these structures. This process is so crucial to understanding text that it is worthwhile spending a little time considering exactly how it works.

Look at the following story beginning:

The man was brought into the large white room. His eyes blinked in the bright light.

Try to picture in your mind the scene so far. Is the man sitting, lying or standing? Is he alone in the room? What sort of room is it? What might this story be going to be about?

Now read the next extract:

'Now, sit there', said the nurse. 'And try to relax.'

Has this altered your picture of the man or of the room? What is this story going to be about?

After the first extract you may have thought the story would be set in a hospital, or perhaps concern an interrogation. There are key words in the brief beginning which trigger off these expectations. After the second extract the possibility of a dentist's surgery may enter your mind, and the interrogation scenario fade.

Each item you read sparks off an idea in your mind, each one of which has its own associated schema, or structure of underlying ideas. It is unlikely, for example, that your picture of the room after the first extract had a plush white carpet on the floor. You construct a great deal from very little information.

Understanding, and in fact, reading, is exactly like this. It is not simply a question of getting a meaning from what is on the page. When you read, you supply a good deal of the meaning to the page. The process is an interactive one, with the resultant learning being a combination of your previous ideas with new ones encountered in this text. This being so, any activities which we use to develop children's understanding from text should emphasize this interaction.

Several activities which emphasize this have been suggested by Lunzer and Gardner (1984) and others, and have the common title of DARTS:- Directed Activities Relating to Texts. These include group cloze, group sequencing and modelling. We shall look briefly at these in turn.

Group Cloze

The cloze exercise consists of a text with several deletions which children have to work together to complete. You might spend a little time discussing the deletions in the following brief text.

The crucial point is that meaning is not in the __ itself, whether the text be literary or otherwise. Rather, meaning arises during the __ between the reader and text. Thus reading is a process, a transaction between reader and text in a given __ context, an event during which meaning evolves.

The solution to the first deletion lies in an application of information which is found elsewhere in the text. The second can be solved by a general understanding of what the text is trying to say. The third, and most open-ended, depends more upon a sense of the style of the passage. Cloze texts prepared for use by children are also likely to feature deletions of these three kinds.

Group Sequencing

The sequencing exercise involves cutting a text up into paragraphs or sentences and then reading to try to reconstruct it. You might try the following sequencing activity. (You will appreciate that the activity works much better if you can physically move around the sections.)

> Some children do not read for meaning in the first place; they simply try to identify the words.
>
> Consider your own experience reading technical literature.
>
> This is often not the case.
>
> Even good readers may fail to get the meaning if they lack experience with the words, the expressions, or the ideas.
>
> You too may sometimes find it possible to identify the words of a sentence without getting the meaning.
>
> When children are reading aloud, it is all too easy to assume that if they identify the words correctly, they are getting the meaning.

You will notice how heavily dependent you are upon small function words which otherwise you take for granted, for example, 'too', 'this'. This activity shows very clearly how readers can be put in a situation of constructing meaning, rather than just getting it.

Modelling

Modelling involves reconstructing the meaning of a text in the form of a picture or a diagram. Try to design a diagram to represent the following text.

> There are two kinds of readers: analyzers and constructors. Either a reader will approach the task by breaking down everything to small component parts, syllables, sounds, letters, or will work in larger units of meaning (phrases or sentences), and will supply the smaller details from the flow of these units.

One possible way of representing this information is as follows:

Reader	Concentrates on				
	sounds	letters	syllables	phrases	sentences
analyzer	✓	✓	✓		
constructor				✓	✓

Notice how the act of creating the diagram almost inevitably leads you into supplying extra information to the text, often called 'reading beyond the lines'.

General Points

Activities such as these, all of which can easily be adapted for use with children of a wide range of ages, have several features in common. They are essentially group activities and the discussion which accompanies them is perhaps their most valuable dimension. They involve readers in active problem-solving, during the course of which they have to generate and test hypotheses. They lay stress upon interaction with texts, and the construction rather than simple reception of meaning. Finally they generate intrinsic interest among readers. Children by and large find them exciting and fun activities. They are certainly a long way from the dull routine of the traditional comprehension exercise.

Using Writing

Writing can, like reading, be an important learning medium, and there are interesting parallels between the two modes. In the same way that reading is sometimes seen as the simple process of transferring meaning from the page into the reader's head, so writing is sometimes viewed as the process of transferring fully formed meaning from the head of the writer onto the page. Neither view does full justice to the processes involved. As we have seen, reading is much more a creative act than a receptive. Similarly the process of writing can be a means of creating and developing meaning, rather than a simple process of retelling it.

In the previous chapter we analyzed the processes which make up writing, and pointed out that it was not as simple a process as it is often thought to be. One common mistake is to think of the writer working out what he wants to say first, and then transcribing these ideas onto paper. This view presents writing as a linear process, that is:

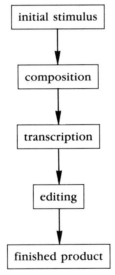

In fact, the process is much more recursive than this. Sometimes ideas might occur in the act of writing; ideas which might then lead to a revision of previously written ideas. Sometimes editing is done before pen is even put to paper, and sometimes revisions themselves are revised. The key to this recursive model of writing is revision, which has a part to play at every stage of the process. A more useful model might look something like this:

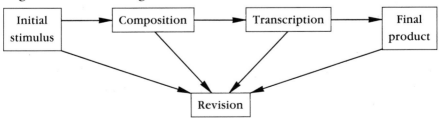

As has been pointed out in previous chapters, seeing writing in this way implies that children are given time and space for the reflection needed for writing. If they are given this space, it is often possible to see evidence of learning through writing in what they produce.

Literacy Across the Curriculum

Clearly reading and writing have a role to play in learning across the whole of the primary curriculum, and not simply in those areas in which attention is specifically devoted to them. Earlier in this chapter you were asked to undertake surveys of the reading and writing done by children over a period of time. Look back at these surveys and list the areas of the curriculum involved. You should find a fairly wide spread of areas.

In this section we shall examine the literacy dimension of several areas of the primary curriculum, and the particular demands that these might make. The areas we shall look at are: science, mathematics and the humanities.

Science

Suggested observation
Observe two children engaged in a science lesson or activity. Note down the uses they make of reading or writing during this activity. Note also any areas which seem to cause them difficulty.

Points to consider
What kind of reading material do the children have to deal with? What would be an ideal method of approaching this material, and how do the children actually approach it? What format of writing are the children expected to produce, and what do they actually produce? Are they given any help with the reading and writing elements of the activity? If so, what does it focus upon?

An example
The following uses of literacy have been observed to occur in science lessons, although obviously not all in any one lesson.

Reading instructions,

workcards;
for background information;
to stimulate interest;
to extend the relevance of activities to the wider world.

Writing records of activities and observations,

reports of work undertaken and results found;
explanations of results;
predictions of future outcomes;
generalizations from work done.

Comment

It is noticeable that the kinds of reading and writing done in science activities tends to involve texts of a different character from those used in other areas of the curriculum. Children's experience of literacy elsewhere may be largely, if not entirely, confined to experience with narrative texts. They read and write stories. The texts they have to read and write in science are generally not narrative, being logical rather than chronological in structure. It can be very difficult for children to adapt their strategies for dealing with texts to the different genres. They clearly need some kind of assistance with this. Yet, as you may have observed for yourself, the assistance they get with their science activities may be confined to a concentration on their science content, rather than on the reading and writing involved in handling this content.

How might the teacher help children deal with the literacy demands of science activities? The key to effective help lies in extended discussion. Teachers often discuss stories with children, both those they read and those they write. This same discussion can help children to come to terms with the problems of handling new text structures. This discussion can be started very early in a child's school career by the teacher occasionally using non-narrative text with children as a variant on the narrative text which usually occupies storytime. Later, activities such as sequencing and modelling, as described earlier, can be used as a focus for discussion specifically concerned with the structure of texts. In writing, teachers can encourage children to stand back from their planning, composition and revision to discuss what they are producing in terms of its structure and the needs of its audience.

Mathematics

Many of the same points which have been made about reading and writing in science apply equally to mathematics. Coping with alternative text structures can, in fact, be more of a problem, partially because there is a tendency for text in mathematics materials to be a disguised form of narrative.

Suggested activity

Choose two or three pages from a mathematics textbook with which you are familiar. Examine carefully the reading which children have to do on these pages. Are there any particular difficulties likely to be caused by this? What do the children have to write in response? Are there any problems with this?

Points to consider

Are the instructions given completely unambiguous?

Can you think of alternative ways of giving them?
(If you can, you might like to try these on children to see if it improves their performance on the mathematics.)

Is there a set format for children's responses?

Is this clearly explained?

If possible, watch some children using these pages and note any points of difficulty they have.

Comment

It is often observed by teachers that children who can actually cope quite easily with the mathematics involved in an activity find it difficult because of the reading they have to do. Which, for example, of the following questions do you think children would find most difficult? You might like to try this out with some children.

What is 32 divided by 4?

Mr Jones, the games teacher, wanted to play two games of football with his class of thirty-two children. This meant he would need four equal sized teams. How many children would there be in each team?

Mary had thirty-two pence. She wanted to share it evenly between her four friends. How much did they get each?

Notice that the mathematics involved in each of these questions is exactly the same. The facility with which children solve the mathematics is, however, greatly affected by the density to which the information is buried in text. Notice also that the two text versions of the question use a form which looks like narrative, but which children have to treat in a totally different way from narrative. With stories they can sit back and enjoy the flow of the language. Here, in contrast, they have to ignore the flow and concentrate on picking out exactly those few pieces of information which matter.

What should the teacher's reaction to this be? It is tempting to reason that, if it is the density of text which causes the problem, then children should be given mathematics questions in a straightforward format, unembedded in text. Unfortunately, of course, mathematics does not occur in real life in neatly separated 'sums', but always embedded in real contexts. We must, therefore, try to ensure that children get experience of dealing with it in this way, and help them with the problems caused by the text. Again, discussion is likely to be the key to helping them towards understanding. A great deal of learning can take place if children are given time to discuss problems they are faced with in mathematics.

Another strategy the teacher can employ is to avoid the temptation to by-pass the text when children have problems. Almost all teachers sometimes tell children who claim they cannot understand what they have to do to 'just multiply that number by that one', or other versions on this theme. This saves a great deal of time, and means the children can get on with the real exercise, the mathematics. Unfortunately, it also misses the real point of the activity and fails to help children apply their literacy to mathematical situations. A better strategy is to ask children to point to the words which they do not understand, and try to help them to understand them, through discussion. Problems are almost always best overcome by facing them directly, rather than skirting round them.

Humanities

By the humanities here we are referring to those areas of the curriculum traditionally called history and geography, or, more modernly, environmental and social studies. Most primary schools cover these areas through project work, which is dealt with specifically in the following section of this chapter. At this point we would like to examine briefly the way in which the teaching of literacy can be grounded in humanities content by the use of DARTS, described earlier in the chapter.

Suggested activity: 1
Read the following text and try to complete it. If possible give it to a group of top juniors to work on.

> Some of the oldest buildings in the north of England are ____ left behind from the days of the Romans and Normans. The houses built by the ____ people have disappeared although if you walk through some of our oldest ____ like Lincoln and Chester you will find buildings which are ____ of years old.
> When the ____ settlers came to the north they had to build some form of ____ against the cold and damp climate. They naturally used the building ____ which was easily obtainable and that was ____. The very first homes would have looked something like a ____ of sticks covered with grass and ____.

Points to notice
In order to complete the text you have to use a variety of clues from the words surrounding the deletions. In doing this you actually increase your knowledge about the subject. Sometimes textual clues lead you to conclusions about content, and at others you may have been forced to look for information elsewhere. This activity develops use of reading *and* subject knowledge.

Suggested activity: 2
Read the following text and try to show the information it contains by means of a diagram. If possible try it out with a group of children.

> Most people are very kind to animals — but some people who like animals sometimes have to kill them. Some people kill animals because they are pests — rats, rabbits and foxes, for instance. Some people kill animals to provide us with food. And some hunt animals for sport. Some hunt animals they can eat, some hunt pests, and some just hunt for pleasure.

Points to consider
Compare your diagram with that below which was produced by a group of 9 and 10-year-olds.

	kill for food	kill for sport	kill as pests	kill to be kind
kind	farmers	xxxxx	farmers foresters	vets foresters
cruel		huntsmen		xxxxx

(When a box is left blank it means the children could not think of anything to put in it. When it contains xxxxx it means they decided that nothing could go in it.)

The children who did this activity have clearly added to the text, reading beyond the lines in the way which was described earlier. By this act of bringing information they already knew to the text which they were reading, it is likely that they learnt a considerable amount from the activity.

Comment

These two activities are only examples of the wide range of applications of DARTS to the humanities area. They have the distinguishing feature of developing at one and the same time the ability to use and respond to reading, and the learning of content knowledge.

Literacy in Project Work

Almost all primary teachers involve their children in some form of project or thematic work. There is obviously a great deal of variation in the extent of this work, with some teachers basing almost their entire curriculum upon it, and others arranging their work so that 'basic skills' such as language, reading and mathematics are taught separately. There is also a great variation in methods of organizing this kind of work. In some classes project work is a whole-class activity, with children all doing the same activities at the same time, while in others it is an individual activity, and children are allowed to follow their own personal lines of enquiry. Of course, there are many other arrangements between these two.

Given the large degree of variation which exists in the practice of project work, it is, perhaps, not very surprising that it has given rise to an increasing amount of concern. Concern has been expressed about the content of project work, and its effectiveness as a context for children's learning. It has been caricatured, somewhat unfairly in many cases, as 'uninvolved copying', and doubt expressed over the extent of children's learning through it.

Yet ideally project work would seem to have a great deal to offer, especially in terms of the development of literacy, as it can combine the two aspects of motivation referred to earlier in the chapter. Children can become really interested in a project, and hence deeply involved in its process. They can also see a clear end-product, and have an incentive to get this product as good as it can be.

In order to capitalize upon the potential of project work two things are necessary. The first is to clearly define what the purpose of the activity is, and the second is to devise a systematic way of carrying it out.

Making Project Work Purposeful

The purpose of project work in terms of literacy development might be seen as developing children's abilities to handle information. The term 'information skills' (Wray, 1985) here embodies much of the practical dimension of literacy, and this term can be defined as those skills involved in the process of locating and using information. This process seems to include six main stages.

1 Defining subject and purpose — that is, specifying what information is required and why. This implies more than the vague 'I want to find out about . . .', which seems all too common in primary school information-handling work. Children need to be encouraged to specify as precisely as possible what it is they want to find out, and what they will do with that information when they have found it.
2 Locating information — finding the required information in libraries, books or elsewhere. This includes knowing how to use the library system to track down likely sources of the information required, how to find information efficiently in books and other sources, but also how to use the most important information resource — other people. Asking the right questions is an important skill which many adults are insufficiently practised in. To this list must also be added the skills of using the various tools of information technology to retrieve needed information. Teletext television, viewdata systems such as Prestel, and computer data-

bases are all extremely useful sources of information in the classroom, but not unless the children possess the requisite skills for using them.

3 Selecting information — choosing the specific information required to meet the purpose identified earlier. Children very often find it very difficult to be selective in the information they extract from books in particular, often resorting to wholesale copying of large extracts. They need to be shown how to match their particular information requirements with what is available, and how to take note of information rather than copy it.

4 Organizing information — synthesizing the information found into a full answer to the original question. Pulling together information from a range of sources can be a very demanding task. It is, however, made a good deal easier if the information need is defined very precisely, as suggested in stage one above. Children need to be positively encouraged to consult a range of information sources in their quest, and then to look for common points, or instances of disagreement in their notes.

5 Evaluating information — evaluating the accuracy, relevance and status of the information found. Children will naturally tend to believe, as will many adults, that everything they read in books is bound to be true. The teacher may need to confront them deliberately with examples of incorrect or biased books if a questioning attitude is to be encouraged. Possibilities for this include out of date books, newspaper reports and advertising material.

6 Communicating results — either using the information for personal purposes or presenting it to others. If children are encouraged to think of a definite audience for their finished work then it will be possible to get them to assess the work's appropriateness for this audience by actually having their work read. The example of this which immediately springs to mind is that of older junior children preparing information booklets for younger children in the same school, although there are many possibilities available for children to prepare reports of particular information — finding activities to pass on to other readers.

Making Project Work Systematic

A project to be of maximum benefit needs to be organized according to a systematic plan and one means of such organization is given below, described in the context of one particular project which was carried out with third year junior school children.

The project was entitled 'Holidays', and arose through interest generated in the class by the children's sharing of their plans for holidays during the coming vacation. Not all the activities undertaken will be described, but only sufficient to give a flavour of the approach.

Devising aims

The first step was for the children, under the guidance but not domination of the teacher, to decide upon what they hoped to achieve during the project. (It was felt important to give the children as much responsibility for planning and running the project as possible. Their commitment was felt to be crucial if the aim of setting skill teaching within a meaningful context was to be achieved.) Two of the goals which were specified for the project were for the children to produce their own holiday brochures for places they had visited on holiday, and their own passports.

Making plans

The next step was to decide, again teacher and pupils together, how to set about achieving the specified aims. It was decided that examples of holiday brochures would have to be obtained as well as other information about specific holiday areas. This involved making arrangements to visit travel agents as well as the local and school libraries. It was also decided that a real passport would be needed and after some discussion one of the children offered to bring in his mum's! Plans were made to visit local post offices to ask for passport application forms. Eventually sufficient of these were obtained to enable each child to fill one in (for practice). All the tasks were delegated and working groups established, each with a timetable within which their particular tasks should be completed.

Implementing plans

In carrying out the plans that had been made the children had to exercise a whole range of location and selection skills. They had to obtain information from books and other printed materials and also by asking questions of people. They had physically to go to where the information they wanted was to be found, either in libraries, post offices or travel agents, and they then had to get the information and bring it back to school. They then had to evaluate the information and put it together into an appropriate form. They had to fill in forms (monitoring each other to ensure they did it correctly), design their passports, and join together descriptive prose and appropriate pictures to produce holiday brochures which retailed information in an accurate and attractive way.

Evaluating progress

The children and the teacher were continually evaluating the success of the process. Regular sessions were held in which groups reported back on their progress. Their form-filling was monitored by other children, and those responsible for obtaining things like printed brochures from travel agents were under a good deal of pressure from their classmates to deliver the goods on time. At the end of the project other children were allowed to read the completed brochures and were asked their opinions as to whether these gave sufficient information to enable a choice of holiday resort to be made and also whether they presented the resorts in a suitably attractive light.

During the project there were several opportunities for instruction in information skills, particularly those of evaluating and synthesizing information from a range of sources. Occasionally groups were brought together who seemed to be having similar problems and direct instruction was employed. Twice the whole class were brought together for some work on critical reading, using a selection of advertisements and newspaper reports. On many more occasions individual children's difficulties were highlighted and attempts made to deal with them on the spot, using a variety of resources. Commercially produced books of exercises on such topics as 'using an index' or 'skimming' were found very useful for this. It was felt that instruction during the project was more likely to have had lasting effect because it was set within a meaningful context. Children could, it was felt, see a purpose in this instruction simply because it was helping them achieve better results in a project in which they were very interested.

After reading this account you might like to compare it with other projects you have been involved in with children. Try to isolate the opportunities for the development of literacy within this project and your own. If you were now planning your project again, would you do it any differently?

Using New Technology

Most primary classes have access to new technology, either a computer, electronic mail system, or merely a teletext television. Observations of the use of technology in primary classrooms tends to suggest, however, that the great opportunities it can offer for the development of literacy are seldom used to the full. A full treatment of the use of the computer in developing literacy is beyond the scope of this chapter, and readers are referred elsewhere (Blows and Wray, 1989). Some time will be spent here, however, examining the possibilities for the development of literacy of the use of word-processing and desktop publishing.

Word-Processing and Desktop Publishing

Word-processing and desktop publishing are, it has been argued (Chandler and Marcus, 1985), enabling devices for children's writing. They enable children to achieve results which otherwise would be impossible or very difficult for them to achieve. Perhaps the most obvious advantage involved in the use of the computer to assist writing is that it is almost guaranteed to produce instant success for its users. All writing done on the computer, whatever its quality, 'looks good'. The computer does not allow differentiation between those with well and poorly developed physical writing skills. Because word-processed text has a professional physical appearance, this is an immediate and important step towards its goal of effective communication.

This in itself would not, of course, be sufficient reason for encouraging children to use the computer to write. Many teachers have also found that word-processing leads to an improved quality in children's writing. Editing and revising texts is made much simpler when it can be done on the screen before committing the writing to paper. This diminution of physical effort encourages children to edit and revise, with consequent improvement in content, style, clarity etc. Word-processing also seems to have a compacting effect on writing, perhaps because it is so easy to delete sections without leaving a trace. By using the computer all writing becomes provisional, and open to addition, extension, rearrangement, deletion and reshaping. This fact cannot help but have profound implications for children's perceptions of the process of writing and its products.

There are a number of other advantages which word-processing and desktop publishing have which make them extremely suitable for use as educational writing environments. The first concerns the purposes for which they are typically used. Most word-processed writing is purposefully produced for other people to read, and its producers are therefore involved in 'public' writing. This adds a dimension of purposefulness to writing which children may occasionally not perceive in their other writing tasks. The public nature of this writing in turn gives children greater incentive to improve its quality and accuracy. Public writing implies also that an audience has to be taken into account. Children who are aware that what they produce is going to be read by a variety of other people can be alerted to the needs of these audiences, and encouraged to reconsider the form and content of their writing in the light of these needs.

The Desktop Publishing Environment

The desktop publishing environment has some features which make it particularly useful for realistic writing formats. One of the most important of these, which the more elaborate software packages have, is the cut and paste facility. By using this, sections of pages can be electronically lifted from one place and moved or copied to another. This is an extension of the provisionality of writing mentioned earlier. Anything children produce can always be changed in a number of ways, and they quickly grasp the power of this, and experiment with format. This is likely to increase their awareness of the effects of different formats on their readers, another important literacy skill.

This facility also allows children to copy faithfully a significant feature of writing environments in the real world. Cut and paste is an essential feature of the production of written products from newspapers to novels, and most children will get some experience of doing this operation with scissors and glue, before using the computer to simplify the process. Using the computer means, of course, that they can experiment with several layouts before finally committing themselves to one. Indeed, they can also easily print out alternative layouts and gain some feedback on their appropriateness and acceptability from other readers. This can only increase their awareness of the demands of different audiences.

Another feature which desktop publishing makes possible is the mixing of text and pictures. Software is now available which enables users to snatch pictures from video players and cameras, and import these as digitized pictures into the desktop publishing environment. Once under the control of the computer software, these pictures can be manipulated in various ways: stretched, enlarged, reduced, rotated, reversed, chopped into pieces and overlaid or interspersed with text. This is a facility of immense potential, which enables users of small personal computers to produce pages which are almost indistinguishable from those of real newspapers. It should not be forgotten that a significant element of literacy has always been the interpretation of pictorial images, and the use of the images to communicate meanings and to supplement the messages conveyed by texts.

One of the features of standard word-processing which is commonly exploited by teachers is the way it encourages cooperation among children. Desktop publishing is even more likely to encourage this, because of the nature of the tasks for which children will often use it, for example, the production of a class or school newspaper. The need for cooperation is built into this task, forcing a sharing approach to writing with task-oriented discussion, collaborative editing and increased sensitivity to the opinions of others.

Word-processing and desktop publishing therefore have immense potential to assist in the development of literacy in children. It would be extremely useful for you to observe a group of children as they use a word-processor. You might try to note down instances which you consider show learning in the children taking part. As their teacher how might you build upon this learning?

Developing the Literacy Habit

In this chapter so far we have concentrated on the developing of children's abilities to get the most from literacy. This has given a somewhat functional feel to our material. In the last section of the chapter, therefore, we want to try to redresss the balance in favour of literacy for enjoyment. We earlier stressed the importance of motivation, and we would clearly aim as teachers to produce children who wanted to use literacy. We would also hope to go farther than this and develop in children a love of literacy for its own sake. Our aim would be to produce children who not only could read and write, but were *readers* and *writers*. We should be satisfied with nothing less.

There are many ways of going about this, most of which have been featured several times already in this book. Uniting these there are some key features which we shall discuss in turn. But first it would be useful to look at the provision for this aspect of literacy in a classroom.

Suggestion for observation
Observe a classroom over a period of at least three days. Note down

the opportunities the children get to develop enjoyment in literacy, and the strategies the teacher uses to encourage this.

Points to consider
How many opportunities are there for enjoyable (rather than purely skill-oriented) use of reading and writing?

What importance seems to be attached to this side of literacy by the teacher and by the children?

Do the children ever see an adult enjoying literacy?

What kind of encouragement are they given by the teacher?

Comments

(a) *Opportunity*
Nobody can learn to enjoy an activity if they are not given the opportunity to do it. This has special relevance to literacy in the upper junior school, when the enjoyment aspect can get neglected. Children may not be told stories as regularly as lower down the school, and they may not get the chance to immerse themselves in their own reading. In writing, with the growth of functional writing, they may miss the opportunities they had earlier of writing about things that really concerned them. All these things need time given to them.

There is no reason at all why upper junior children should not be told stories as regularly as younger children, and every reason why they should. Hearing stories can introduce them to language and ideas which they otherwise may not encounter. Stories can spark off a whole range of interesting, creative work involving all areas of the curriculum, and can provide the perfect context for the sustained interaction with literature which we discussed earlier. At this stage it is likely that the teacher will read longer novels in serial form, but these should be interspersed with short stories. Children will also benefit from being allowed to share their own favourite stories with others in the class, and this 'sharing' time might be a built-in feature of their classroom week.

These children also need time to immerse themselves in books. If private reading is left to odd spare moments then children are unlikely to get the time to be 'lost in a book', and many of those who work fairly slowly (and who may need to experience the pleasure of reading the most) may never get chance at all. Many teachers set aside special times, perhaps once a day, when everyone in the class reads a book. These times are variously called:

> USSR   — Uninterrupted Sustained Silent Reading,
> ERIC   — Everyone Reading In Class,
> SQIRT — Sit Quietly, It's Reading Time.

With writing, children will benefit from being given the freedom to explore ideas in writing, rather than writing always being done to the order of the teacher. To this end, many teachers and schools have found that writing corners are a useful idea. A part of the classroom (it varies from a corner to an empty stock cupboard) is set aside, and provided with a range of writing implements and media (from felt tip pens to a typewriter) for children to write with as they wish. The corner also has space for the display of finished writing or writing in progress. Sometimes a group of children is elected as a writing corner committee, and formulates rules for the use of the corner (with appropriate sanctions for transgressors). Teachers have found that corners like this are heavily used by children and really do seem to encourage enjoyment in writing.

(b) *Status*

It is little use supplying children with the opportunities to engage enjoyably with literacy if the underlying message of the classroom is that these things are not really as important as 'real work', or that the enjoyable side of them is not the most important thing. Teachers can give this impression in all sorts of ways, for example:

> The opportunities for silent reading occur only at the end of the day or session, when the real work is finished.
>
> These opportunities are regularly lost when something more important comes up.
>
> The teacher interrupts them with requests to hear readers, or to mark work.
>
> The teacher's first reaction to writing done because it was an enjoyable way of exploring feelings, memories etc. is to say something like, 'That is neat', or 'What a lot of mistakes!'

This list could obviously be extended. Children are very good at picking up from the tiniest of clues what it is that their teacher really values, and these are the things they will try hardest to achieve. The enjoyment of literacy needs to be given a high status, both explicitly by the teacher regularly telling children how important it is, and implicitly by arranging the classroom environment so that its importance is demonstrated.

(c) *Models*

For many children the message in the classroom is 'do as I say, not as I do', and they may rarely actually see any adults enjoying literacy. If the teacher tells children that reading and writing are enjoyable, and even gives them high status opportunities to engage in these things, but never actually shows them that he/she enjoys them too, the children may get the message that reading and writing are not important for adults but only in school. To counteract this, teachers need to ensure that there are occasions, as regular as is possible, when:

> they are seen reading, with enjoyment, material that they choose for pleasure;
> they discuss their own favourite reading with the children;
> they write extended pieces;
> they share things they have written at home with the children.

Teachers often feel a little uneasy about doing some of these things, aware that outsiders may not count them as really working. There is, however, a powerful rationale for them, which teachers might explain with conviction to these outsiders. Certainly the modelling of literate behaviour should never be apologized for, since it can have a tremendous impact upon children's achievement of full literacy.

Conclusion

This chapter has covered a great deal of ground and has, hopefully, demonstrated among other things that the development of literacy needs to be given as much attention in the top junior years as earlier in children's school careers. A great deal has been written about literacy in the early years, but the later years have tended to be neglected in the past. Yet, as this chapter shows, there are a vast number of issues to consider both in the development of reading and writing. And, of course, the process does not stop here. Literacy remains an important issue for secondary schooling too, but that is beyond the scope of this book.

Chapter 7

Conclusion

This book has been concerned with the development of literacy before and during the years of primary schooling. This time is a very exciting one for children's development and it makes important intrinsic demands upon their literacy. It is also a time of preparation and it is the nature of what is being prepared for and its implications for primary practice which we shall consider briefly in our conclusion, picking out two major implications only.

There are two aspects to this preparation. One is that children will leave primary school to go on to other stages of education. A second is that children will themselves become adults in a world which may be significantly different from that of their parents and teachers. We shall discuss these two aspects in turn.

To the Secondary School and Beyond

Generally, as children progress through the education system, the demands increase upon them to use their literacy for study purposes, often in situations where they have little support from their teachers. Those who progress to higher education will be expected to do most of their studying independently, and studying invariably means the use of literacy. These developments mean that pupils and students need gradually to become able to take more and more responsibility for their own use of literacy. This process can begin much earlier, in the primary school.

Good teachers have always realized that part of their role is to make themselves redundant, in the sense that it involves encouraging children to be more and more independent in their learning. There is little point in teachers encouraging children to be dependent upon them because, inevitably, there will come a time when children have to operate without the help of the teacher. Yet it is very common for teachers somehow to produce children who find it hard to operate on their own. You might be able to recall instances from your observation of classrooms when children showed that their use of literacy was dependent upon the teacher.

Examples you might have thought of include:

Children asking for precise instructions as to how to set out work, for example, 'Do we put the date?'

Children asking the teacher to spell words for them — words which may already be in their spelling books or on the classroom wall.

Children waiting for a signal before they turn the page in the book they are reading to their teacher.

Children doing project work using teacher-prepared work cards to guide their research.

Instances like these are not wrong in themselves, and there may be perfectly good reasons for any of them. What is worrying is when they form part of a consistent pattern of child dependence upon teacher.

How might the teacher begin to develop independence in children's use of literacy? This will clearly vary with the age of the child, but some positive ways may include:

Stressing strategies for dealing with literacy which children can use themselves, for example, the use of word-banks and dictionaries in writing, simple note-taking techniques in reading for information, educated guesses in spelling and in reading activities.

Organizing group work so that children can learn to work together and help each other.

Abandoning restrictive rules about setting out etc., or making sure that children know these only matter in final draft writing which will be published.

The Future of Literacy

The world is constantly changing, and the pace of change has undoubtedly hotted up as this century has progressed. There can be little doubt that this pace will continue to accelerate. What are the likely implications for the nature of literacy and for its development in primary schools?

The first point which needs to be made here is that attempting to predict the future is a notoriously uncertain business. Predictions are always risky things, and they have proved especially so with regard to the spread and the impact of new technology. Twenty years ago few people would have confidently predicted the situation we have now in the United Kingdom, namely:

> The United Kingdom having a higher proportion of computer-owning homes than any other country in the world.

> The ready availability of cheap, easy to use, powerful microcomputers, some no bigger than a telephone directory.

> Every school in the United Kingdom possessing at least one computer, and the majority more than one.

> A substantial number of primary school children routinely experiencing at school a range of sophisticated uses of the computer, from word-processing to the manipulation of data.

Most people would have underestimated the pace of developments in these areas, and their prediction of future developments proved too cautious. On the other hand, however, many predictions made twenty years ago have subsequently proved over-ambitious, optimistic or simply off target. Things which were predicted, but have not yet (and may not ever) come about include:

> Classrooms will consist of ranks of personal computers, one per child, with each child following an individualized programme of instruction, guided and monitored by the computer.

> Books will become obsolete, their function as stores of information being taken over by computers. (This can be compared with the claim of the inventor Thomas Edison in 1913 that film would 'completely replace the book in New York schools by the end of this decade'.)

> Most children will not need to go to school, but will instead follow programmes of study on their own computers in their own homes.

It is clear from the inaccuracies of these predictions that the future is not what it used to be. How does this affect literacy?

The most important point to be made is that the fundamental features of literacy have not, and probably will not change. The processes of reading and writing are basically the same whether you perform them using books, pencils and paper and typewriters, or computer screens and word processors. What changes are the skills you need to access those processes. The manipulation of information stored on a computer demands the use of different skills from those involved in the use of a book. Similarly, writing on a word processor uses different skills from writing with a pen. In both cases, however, the processes of comprehension and composition are probably the same.

The impact of new technology on literacy, therefore, is more a widening of the concept than a basic change. Schools need to understand this widening and prepare their pupils for it. How might this be achieved? Several things immediately suggest themselves.

(a) Children need to get experience of consulting computerized information stores. These range from databases held on microcomputers to viewdata systems accessed through television or the telephone system.

(b) Children need experience of reading and extracting information from computer screens. There are several features which screens have which books usually do not, for example, coloured, flashing or moving text. Evidence suggests that children find it no more difficult to understand text on a computer screen than on a page, but they may well need to be taught to interpret the extra information which features on the screen can convey.

(c) Children need experience of creating their own texts on a computer. Word-processing has been used very successfully with primary school children and seems to have many positive effects upon their command of the writing process.

Giving children these experiences has, of course, major implications for the level of resourcing of schools in terms of computers etc. It will be difficult to achieve these satisfactorily if each child has a computer in his class for one afternoon a week only. At the very least it will be necessary for there to be a computer permanently stationed in each class, although even this is not really adequate.

Finale

To finish the book we should like to return to a question we posed in the first chapter. Then we asked you to attempt a definition of literacy. If you have worked through the rest of the book you may have found your definition has changed. You might be interested now to compare your definition with that we have been working to throughout the book.

Literacy is the ability and willingness to exercise mastery over the processes used in contemporary society to encode, decode and evaluate meanings conveyed by printed symbols.

The fostering of this is, we believe, *the* major aim of the education process. Primary education cannot be expected to achieve this entirely, but it has a crucial part to play. We hope this book has helped you better understand and develop your role in assisting all the children in your care, now and in the future, to become literate.

Bibliography

Beginning to study any area of interest in education is a little like making a large snowball and, in the case of literacy, a very large snowball indeed. You read one book which refers you to several others. Each of these refers you to others still, and so the process continues. It is very easy to become overwhelmed.

The main purpose of this book has been to introduce you to some of the important ideas and practices in the teaching of literacy, but it does not offer, of course, a complete treatment of the area. If you wish to take things further, the following list of sources would be an excellent next layer for your snowball.

BLOOM, W. (1987) *Partnership with Parents in Reading*, London, Hodder and Stoughton

Examines the research done on the involvement of parents in the teaching of reading and makes several very practical recommendations and suggestions for ways forward in this area.

BLOWS, M. and WRAY, D. (Eds) (1989) *Using Computers Effectively*, Leamington Spa, Scholastic Publications

Contains several very practically oriented chapters on how to get the best out of the computer in the primary classroom. Specially useful for its discussion of the role of the word-processor.

de CASTELL, S., LUKE, A. and EGAN, K. (Eds) (1986) *Literacy, Society and Schooling*, Cambridge, Cambridge University Press

A collection of readings about the nature, history and social background of literacy. The book is distinguished from other volumes on this subject by its close attention to the teaching implications of its discussions.

Bibliography

FERREIRO, E. and TEBEROSKY, A. (1983) *Literacy Before Schooling*, London, Heinemann Educational

An early venture into the growing study of emergent literacy. Charts the development of literacy processes from a Piagetian, psychological perspective.

GRAVES, D. (1983) *Writing: Teachers and Children at Work*, London, Heinemann

The seminal work on children's writing. Introduced several crucial terms and concepts to the theory and practice of writing development, especially the idea of the 'process approach'.

HALL, N. (1987) *The Emergence of Literacy*, London, Hodder and Stoughton

A review of research and insights into the relatively new field of literacy before schooling. Charts several features of environments which can aid the development of literacy.

HALL, N. (Ed) (1989) *Writing with Reason*, London, Hodder and Stoughton

A collection of case studies of children using writing in very purposeful ways. The book shows conclusively that children, when they see the purpose of what they are doing, are capable of more than might have been supposed.

HARSTE, J., WOODWARD, V., and BURKE, C. (1984) *Language Stories and Literacy Lessons*, London, Heinemann Educational

An important attempt to account for the social basis for the development of early literacy. Fascinating too for its close look at young children in the act of being literate. Readers never look at young children in quite the same way again.

HEATH, S. B. (1983) *Ways With Words*, Cambridge, Cambridge University Press

Reports an anthropological study of the development of literacy in contrasting communities in North America. Gives important attention to the role of stories told within a culture and about it.

LUNZER, E. and GARDNER, K. (1984) *Learning from the Written Word*, London, Heinemann Educational

A follow up to an earlier investigation into the use of reading to learn. Puts forward many useful and practical suggestions for developing this area.

WATERLAND, L. (1985) *Read With Me*, Stroud, Thimble Press

A very small book which has become one of the most widely read books on teaching reading. Describes the author's school's approach to teaching reading which eschews the use of a reading scheme and uses 'real' books and an apprenticeship approach.

WRAY, D. (1985) *Teaching Information Skills Through Project Work*, London, Hodder and Stoughton

Gives a rationale for the use of project work as a means of developing literacy and, in particular, the ability to locate and use information. Gives a practical framework for development and includes four case studies of project work in action.

WRAY, D. (Ed) (1988) *Developing Children's Writing*, Leamington Spa, Scholastic Publications

A collection of chapters on aspects of writing, ranging from writing in the early stages to classroom environments, via the use of new technology. Practical suggestions are in the foreground, but the book sets these into a coherent theoretical background.

References

BEARD, R. (1983) *Children's Writing in the Primary School*, London, Hodder and Stoughton.

BLOOM, W. (1987) *Partnership with Parents in Reading*, London, Hodder and Stoughton.

BLOOM, W., MARTIN, T., and WATERS, M. (1988) *Managing to Read*, London, Mary Glasgow.

BLOWS, M. and WRAY, D. (1989) *Using Computers Effectively* , Leamington Spa, Scholastic Publications.

BRANSFORD, J. and JOHNSON, M. (1973) 'Consideration of some problems in comprehension' in CHASE, W. (Ed) *Visual Information Processing*, New York, Academic Press.

CHANDLER, D. and MARCUS, S. (1985) *Computers and Literacy*, Milton Keynes, Open University Press.

CRYSTAL, D. (1986) *Listen to Your Child*, London, Penguin.

DE CASTELL, S., LUKE, A., and EGAN, K. (1986) *Literacy, Society and Schooling*, Cambridge, Cambridge University Press.

DEPARTMENT OF EDUCATION AND SCIENCE (1988) *English For Ages 5 to 11*, London, HMSO.

FERREIRO, E. (1986) 'Literacy development: Psychogenesis', paper presented at World Congress on Reading, London.

FERREIRO, E. and TEBEROSKY, A. (1983) *Literacy Before Schooling*, Portsmouth, New Hampshire, Heinemann Educational.

FREIRE, P. (1972) *Pedagogy of the Oppressed*, London, Penguin.

HALL, N. (1987a) 'Printed on the mind', *Child Education*, 64, 5, pp. 11–13.

HALL, N. (1987b) *The Emergence of Literacy*, London, Hodder and Stoughton.

HALL, N. (1988) 'Nursery children's views about reading and writing' in ANDERSON, C. (Ed) *Reading: the ABC and Beyond*, London, Macmillan Education.

HALL, N., MAY, E., MOORES, J., SHEARER, J., and WILLIAMS, S. (1987) 'The literate home corner' in SMITH, P. (Ed) *Parents and Teachers Together*, London, Macmillan Education.

HALL, N., HERRING, G., HENN, H., and CRAWFORD, L. (1989) *Parental Views on Writing and the Teaching of Writing*, Manchester, Manchester Polytechnic.

References

HARSTE, J., WOODWARD, V., and BURKE, C. (1984) *Language Stories and Literacy Lessons*, Portsmouth, New Hampshire, Heinemann Educational.

HEATH, S. B. (1983) *Ways With Words*, Cambridge, Cambridge University Press.

HOLDAWAY, D. (1979) *The Foundations of Literacy*, Sydney, Ashton Scholastic.

HUGHES, M. and GRIEVE, R. (1983) 'On asking children bizarre questions' in DONALDSON, M., GRIEVE, R., and PRATT, C. (Eds) *Early Childhood Development and Education*, Oxford, Blackwell.

KINNEAVY, J. (1971) *A Theory of Discourse*, New Jersey, Prentice Hall.

LUNZER, E. and GARDNER, K. (1979) *The Effective Use of Reading*, London, Heinemann Educational.

LUNZER, E. and GARDNER, K. (1984) *Learning From the Written Word*, London, Heinemann Educational.

MEEK, M. (1982) *Learning to Read*, London, The Bodley Head.

MERRITT, J. (1973) *Perspectives on Reading*, Milton Keynes, Open University Press.

PETERS, R. (1966) *Ethics and Education*, London, George Allen and Unwin.

RUMELHART, D. (1984) 'Understanding understanding', in FLOOD, J. (Ed) *Understanding Reading Comprehension*, Newark, Delaware, International Reading Association.

SMITH, F. (1978) *Reading*, Cambridge, Cambridge University Press.

SMITH, F. (1983) *Essays into Literacy*, London, Heinemann Educational.

SMITH, F. (1988) *Joining the Literacy Club*, London, Heinemann Educational.

WATERLAND, L. (1985) *Read With Me*, Stroud, Thimble Press.

WEAVER, C. (1988) *Reading Process and Practice*, Portsmouth, New Hampshire, Heinemann Educational.

WELLS, G. (1987) *The Meaning Makers*, London, Heinemann Educational.

WRAY, D., HUMBERSTONE, J., and CLAXTON, J. (1989) *Learning Through Talking*, Lancaster, Centre for Educational Research and Development, University of Lancaster.

WRAY, D. (1985) *Teaching Information Skills Through Project Work*, London, Hodder and Stoughton.

WRAY, D. (1988) 'Literacy: the information dimension' in ANDERSON, C. (Ed) *Reading: the ABC and Beyond*, London, Macmillan Education.

Index

Index